T0347058

ISTANBUL
CULT RECIPES

ISTANBUL
CULT RECIPES

POMME LARMOYER

PHOTOGRAPHS BY AKIKO IDA AND PIERRE JAVELLE
ILLUSTRATIONS BY ZEINA ABIRACHED
STYLING BY SABRINA FAUDA-RÔLE

murdoch books
Sydney | London

PREFACE

Istanbul welcomed me into its vast embrace early one morning. Arriving from the East by train into Haydarpaşa Station, I had my feet in Asia and the Bosphorus and Europe in front of me. The 'City of Cities' was all around me. For those who love travel, Istanbul is Byzantium; ancient and yet ultra-modern, imposing and incredibly endearing. 'Are you lost? We will come with you. Are you curious? Come and explore.' The food is like the city: endless, generous, varied and festive. There is as much to see in the former Constantinople as there is to discover in its food – and that's a lot. The city's dishes are so diverse, surprising and refined that if you are new to Istanbul, you might wonder how you could have overlooked it for so long. Eating there is like putting together a beautiful mosaic because Ottoman cuisine is a vast gastronomic culture that spans epochs and influences from Europe, the Middle East, Central Asia and the Mediterranean – it evokes journeys, histories and peoples. There is the food of the street: rich and frankly addictive; the food served in homes and cafés: simple, healthy and fresh. The contemporary cuisine is elegant and attractive – the good that comes when the new appropriates the old. And this sums up Istanbul: a crossroads, a diversity of styles, cultures and rituals. It is Europe and Asia, the sea and the land, a megalopolis and individual neighbourhoods, tradition and the new, Turkish, Greek, Jewish, Armenian and Kurdish neighbourhoods, secular here, religious there. Little lanes in the bazaar and, just opposite, the wide and busy İstiklâl Caddesi. Istanbul is a simit food cart and a rakı (anise-flavoured spirit) apéritif on a terrace overlooking the Bosphorus, and in the middle and all around is the strait, the Golden Horn, the sea.

Istanbul shares with its residents and visitors alike a great love affair with food. You will always find something to eat in the city, whatever the time of day or night. There are morning dishes, midday dishes, four o'clock dishes (tea with a börek), evening meals, dishes for before the game (a little dürüm?), after the game (here you go, an islak burger), for later at night (go on, a plate of mantı), for on the way home (a tripe soup or sandwich at five in the morning!).

One thing to remember when exploring the city's food culture is that almost every dish has its own neighbourhood, and a best address at which to enjoy it. This makes for a long list of places to stop for lunch, dinner, afternoon tea, a snack on the run or just a little treat to help get back one's strength. There are the *kahvaltı salonu*, dedicated to breakfast; the *lokanta*, cafeteria-style restaurants that serve ready-made dishes; and the *meyhane*, taverns that serve meze, fish and rakı. The *ocakbaşı* is the restaurant for grilled meats; the *çorbacı* is the soup bar; the *kahvehane* is where you drink coffee; the *pidecisi* sells pide (pizza); the *köfteci* köfte (meatballs); the *kebabcı* kebabs; the *mantıcı* mantı (dumplings); and the *işkembeci* offal and tripe dishes. Not to mention the *yufkacı* (where you can buy thin yufka pastry), the *muhallebici* (the place to go for desserts), the *balık restoran* (oyster bar), the *fırın* (bakery)…

ARE YOU HUNGRY? WELCOME TO İSTANBUL.

TABLE OF CONTENTS

AT THE KAHVALTI SALONU

BREAKFAST
page 8

THE MEYHANE TABLE

MEZE AND FISH
page 24

LOKANTA, KÖFTECI, KEBABCI

SOUPS, MEATS AND RICE
page 78

AT HOME

FAMILY RECIPES
page 132

STREET FOOD
page 180

TURKISH DELIGHTS

SWEET THINGS
page 206

APPENDICES

INGREDIENTS AND RECIPE INDEX
page 258

AT THE KAHVALTI SALONU

BREAKFAST

The traditional breakfast is the *kahvaltı* – literally *kahve altı*, or 'under (before) the coffee', which is to say the food you eat before drinking a coffee. It is actually the most complete meal of the day – the equivalent of a brunch. In Istanbul it is quite acceptable to eat *kahvaltı* late, even in the afternoon. The main thing is allowing the time to savour it. Sunday is often an occasion for lingering around a well-laden table, and the *kahvaltı salonu* (restaurants specialising in breakfast) are full to bursting all day long.

On the *kahvaltı* table are sliced tomatoes and cucumbers, olives, cheeses (beyaz peynir, a 'white' cheese similar to feta; dil peyniri, mild and stringy; kaşar, a firmer cheese, made from sheep's or goat's milk …), bread, jam, kaymak (a sort of clotted cream made from buffalo's milk), honey … as well as more substantial dishes.

FATIH - OLD ISTANBUL

In the west part of Fatih (the municipality of old Istanbul) are **Balat** and **Fener**, the old Jewish and Greek quarters, which are among the most beautiful in the city. Lose yourself in the alleyways that go up and down, among the red roofs of the little houses that are sometimes coloured and often rundown. Unpretentious, poor in parts, trendier in others, these rapidly evolving neighbourhoods always come across as a world apart within Istanbul. *Agora Meyhanesi 1890* (*Mürselpaşa Caddesi 185, Ayvansaray, Fatih*), a huge old tavern that was reopened in 2014, successfully carries on the spirit of the original establishment (which dates from 1890), with its vintage objects, its in-house products and above all its cooking, faithful to the Greeks who originally founded the Agora.

Not too far away (if you don't get lost, but you will get lost and that's the whole point), *Asitane* restaurant (*Kariye Camii Sokak No: 6, Edirnekapı*) reconnects with the Ottoman gastronomic tradition, the cuisine of the empire's palaces, with their thousands of slightly forgotten recipes, some of which are revived here. The establishment is next to the old Byzantine **Church of the Holy Saviour in Chora**, with its beautiful proportions and sublime mosaics (now a museum).

From Haliç (the Golden Horn), if you make your way towards the bazaars and Sultanahmet, you will go past Kadir Has University, which is home to the **chef school restaurant** of the Istanbul Culinary Institute (*Kadir Has Caddesi, Cibali*). Go in for a good lunch in a university atmosphere, made by the chefs of tomorrow.

4   Now head towards the **Egyptian Bazaar**. There is everything to see here, way beyond the old covered spice bazaar. Inside, you do not know where to stop – which pile of saffron, pepper, paprika, soaps? – but do spend a moment at *Ucuzcular* (Mısır Çarşısı İçi No: 51), which is highly

5   recommended for the quality of its spices. Once outside, it is hard to miss *Kurukahveci Mehmet Efendi* (Tahmis Sokak No: 66, in front of the entrance to the Egyptian Bazaar), a master coffee roaster. This is first because you can smell it from 40 metres away; next, because all you can see is the permanent line of people queueing for its little packets of coffee. Line up like everyone else!

Wander over towards the **Grand Bazaar**. If the spice bazaar seemed small, the Grand Bazaar will not. It is hard not to get lost here, or even find what you are looking for, but never mind. The place is worth the endless toing and froing, and obviously you will end up finding something.

6   You can always sit down for 5 minutes at *Café Ethem Tezçakar*, (Halıcılar Caddesi, No: 61/63). This coffee shop, in the middle of the central alleyway of the Grand Bazaar, is not large and fills up quickly. The coffee? It is delicious. And the café is a well-chosen spot for watching the happenings of the bazaar ebb and flow, before heading back into the crowd yourself to visit *Abdulla* (Halıcılar Caddesi, No: 58/60), the shop opposite that is devoted to bath products and where everything is beautiful, starting with the soaps.

If you feel a little peckish, there is no lack of good *pidecisi* (pide-makers) and *köftecisi* (köfte-

7   makers) in Fatih. Some are institutions, such as *Sultanahmet köftecisi* (Divanyolu Caddesi 12/A, Sultanahmet), a local cafeteria worth discovering for its köfte and irmik helvası.

Feel like some green? Go to the extreme southwest of the municipality to see the **Yedikule market gardens** (see page 172) – the Kazlıçeşme metro station will drop you there. Forget the traffic running right beside it and stop at the old city gates, at the foot of the old battlements – built in the fifth century, no less. The market garden tradition has been carried on here for centuries. Not so long ago, the local yield met Istanbul's needs. Not any more (after an enormous population boom), but it remains important, surprising and a pleasure to see. Heading down along the Marmara Sea, the small square of the old Armenian quarter of **Samatya** is a lovely place for a quiet seafood lunch, away from the bustle of the city.

SIMIT AND TURKISH TEA

simit and çay

Simit is *the* bread of Istanbul. It is its beacon, its symbol, a safe bet – sold everywhere for a single lira. It even travels with its street vendors in little red carts that look like the old trams that run along Istiklâl Caddesi, Istanbul's main pedestrian and commercial thoroughfare. You could eat this sesame-covered twisted crown with a sweet aftertaste all day long. That's what Istanbulites do in any case.

Preparation time: 15 minutes
Resting time: 1 hour 15 minutes
Cooking time: 25 minutes
Makes 3 simit
2 teaspoons dried yeast
200 g (7 oz/1⅓ cups) strong flour
1 teaspoon salt
1 teaspoon caster (superfine) sugar
125 ml (4 fl oz/½ cup) water
90 ml (3 fl oz) pekmez (grape molasses) (see note)
sesame seeds

Blend the yeast with a little lukewarm water in a small bowl, and leave to stand for 15 minutes. In a large bowl, mix together the flour, salt, sugar, yeast mixture and water (do not let the salt and yeast come in direct contact with each other) until a sticky dough forms. Turn out onto a lightly floured work surface, and knead for a few minutes until smooth. Transfer to a clean bowl, and cover with a damp tea towel (dish towel). Leave to rise in a warm, draught-free place for 1 hour, or until doubled in size (a warming drawer in the oven at a very low setting – 30°C/85°F – is ideal). Preheat the oven to 200°C (400°F). Knock back the dough, and quickly knead until smooth and elastic once again. Divide into three 100 g (3½ oz) balls, and shape each one into a long sausage, about 60 cm (24 inches) long. Fold each sausage in two and twist along the length, before shaping into a ring (overlap the ends about 3 cm/1¼ inches). Set out two small plates. Pour the pekmez into one and the sesame seeds into the other. Dip each dough ring first in the pekmez, then in the sesame seeds, until well coated. Arrange the simit on a baking tray, and bake for 25 minutes, or until golden brown.

Tea is the most-consumed drink in Turkey. What's more, the country is one of the world's leading tea producers. Tea is the first brew of the morning, the one that welcomes a friend to the home and the one that you see carried around the streets of Istanbul on round trays all day long, by vendors who are constantly in motion.

Preparation time: 5 minutes
Infusion time: 15 minutes
1 teaspoon loose black tea per person
granulated sugar, to taste

Fill the lower part of the *çaydanlık* (Turkish teapot) with water, and put the tea in the upper part. Place the teapot over medium heat. After the water comes to the boil, pour some over the tea, and leave it to infuse for 15 minutes (keeping the lower part of the teapot over low heat; the water must remain hot). Pour the tea into a glass until about one-third full, and top up with boiling water. Sweeten with sugar.

Note: Pekmez, or grape molasses, is made from grape must that has been reduced to a syrup, to intensify the sweetness. It is available from Turkish or other Middle Eastern and Mediterranean food shops, or online from specialist food suppliers.

> TRADITIONAL BLACK TEA, WHICH HAS A RED TINT WHEN SERVED IN GLASSES, IS MADE IN A TWO-TIERED TEAPOT CALLED A 'ÇAYDANLIK': THE TOP PART CONTAINS THE TEA AND THE LOWER PART THE WATER.

PLAIN MILK BUNS
sade poğoça

These little sweet buns (pronounced 'po-otcha') are eaten at breakfast and even lunchtime, or at the four o'clock tea break. They are even better when served hot.

Preparation time: 15 minutes
Resting time: 2 hours
Cooking time: 20 minutes
Serves 4 (8 buns)

DOUGH

20 g (¾ oz) fresh yeast or 1½ teaspoons dried
125 ml (4 fl oz/½ cup) lukewarm water
500 g (1 lb 2 oz/3⅓ cups) strong flour
1 teaspoon salt
1 teaspoon caster (superfine) sugar
120 ml (4 fl oz/½ cup) lukewarm milk
60 ml (2 fl oz/¼ cup) olive oil
1 egg yolk, lightly beaten
1 small handful black and golden sesame seeds

In a small bowl, dissolve the yeast in the lukewarm water and leave to stand for a few minutes. Mix together the flour, salt and sugar in a large bowl, then add the yeast mixture, milk and olive oil. Continue mixing until a sticky dough forms. Turn out onto a lightly floured work surface, and knead for a few minutes until smooth and elastic. Shape into a ball, and transfer to a clean bowl. Cover with a damp tea towel (dish towel). Leave to rise in a warm, draught-free place for 2 hours, or until doubled in size. Preheat the oven to 180°C (350°F). Quickly knead the dough until smooth and elastic once again. Take a portion the size of an orange (about 100 g/3½ oz), and shape into a ball. Brush the top with a little of the egg yolk, and decorate with sesame seeds. Repeat with the rest of the dough until you have eight buns. Arrange the buns on a baking tray, and bake for about 20 minutes until golden.

Personal variation: Add a handful of currants to the dough.

WITH CHEESE

1 quantity milk bun dough (see left)
200 g (7 oz) beyaz peynir (see note) or
    feta cheese, crumbled
1 egg yolk, lightly beaten
1 small handful black and golden sesame seeds

Make the dough according to the instructions at left. Preheat the oven to 180°C (350°F). Quickly knead the dough until smooth once again. Take a portion the size of an orange (about 100 g/3½ oz), flatten it into a circle about 12 cm (4½ inches) across, and place a tablespoon of the crumbled cheese in the middle. Fold the dough over into a semicircle, seal the edges by pressing them together with your fingers, brush the top with egg yolk and decorate with sesame seeds. Repeat until you have eight buns. Arrange on a baking tray, and bake for 20 minutes.

Note: Beyaz peynir is a Turkish cheese made from sheep's, goat's or cow's milk. It is brined, and often unpasteurised. You should be able to find it in Turkish food shops, but feta is a good substitute if you cannot track it down.

WITH HERBS

1 quantity milk bun dough (see left)
about 30 pitted green olives, chopped
3–4 tablespoons fresh or dried thyme leaves
1 egg yolk, lightly beaten
1 small handful black and golden sesame seeds

Make the dough according to the instructions at left. Preheat the oven to 180°C (350°F). Add the olives and thyme to the dough, then knead quickly until smooth. Shape into eight balls the size of an orange (about 100 g/3½ oz each). Brush the tops with egg yolk, and decorate with sesame seeds. Arrange the buns on a baking tray, and bake for 20 minutes.

STUFFED FLATBREAD
gözleme

The morning crêpe, the Turkish pancake, in short. You can add 2 tablespoons plain or Greek-style yoghurt to the dough to make it softer.

Preparation time: 15 minutes
Resting time: 2 hours
Cooking time: 10 minutes
Serves 4 (about 12 gözleme)

DOUGH
20 g (¾ oz) fresh yeast or 1½ teaspoons dried
125 ml (4 fl oz/½ cup) lukewarm water
500 g (1 lb 2 oz/3⅓ cups) strong flour
1 teaspoon salt
1 teaspoon caster (superfine) sugar
125 ml (4 fl oz/½ cup) lukewarm milk
60 ml (2 fl oz/¼ cup) olive oil

In a small bowl, dissolve the yeast in the lukewarm water, and leave to stand for a few minutes. Mix together the flour, salt and sugar in a large bowl, then add the yeast mixture, milk and olive oil. Continue mixing until a sticky dough forms. Turn out onto a lightly floured work surface, and knead for a few minutes until smooth and elastic. Shape into a ball, and transfer to a clean bowl. Cover with a damp tea towel (dish towel). Leave to rise in a warm, draught-free place for 2 hours, or until doubled in size. Quickly knead the dough until smooth and elastic once again. Remove a piece about the size of an egg, and shape into a ball. Using a rolling pin, roll out the dough into a circle about 12 cm (4½ inches) across and place a tablespoon of your choice of filling (cooled to room temperature if needed) in the middle. Fold the dough over to form a semicircle, and seal the edges by pressing them together with your fingers. Continue in this way until all the dough has been used. Cook the gözleme one at a time in a hot crêpe pan or large frying pan over medium heat (do not add any fat or oil) for 5 minutes on each side, or until golden brown and cooked through.

CHEESE FILLING
250 g (9 oz) beyaz peynir (Turkish white cheese,
see page 14) or feta cheese, crumbled
1 large handful flat-leaf (Italian) parsley

Mix together the cheese and parsley until evenly combined, and use to fill the gözleme.

SPINACH FILLING
olive oil
1 small onion, finely chopped
250 g (9 oz/5½ cups) baby English spinach leaves
80 g (2¾ oz) beyaz peynir (Turkish white cheese,
see page 14) or feta cheese, crumbled
1 tablespoon pul biber (Aleppo pepper) or
other chilli flakes (optional)

Heat a little olive oil in a large frying pan over medium heat. Add the onion and sauté for 5 minutes, or until soft and translucent. Add the spinach and cook, stirring, for 3 minutes. Gently stir through the crumbled cheese and chilli flakes (if using), and cook for another minute.

POTATO FILLING
3 all-purpose potatoes (such as desiree)
25 g (1 oz) butter
1 small onion, finely chopped
1 tablespoon tomato paste (concentrated purée)
a few flat-leaf (Italian) parsley sprigs, chopped
1 tablespoon dried mint

Peel and halve the potatoes. Cook in plenty of salted boiling water until tender to the point of a knife. Drain and mash well; set aside. Melt the butter in a large frying pan over medium heat. Add the onion and sauté for about 5 minutes until soft. Add the tomato paste, mashed potato, parsley, dried mint and a little salt. Mix to bind together well.

FRIED EGGS AND SUCUK

sucuklu yumurta

Sucuk (pronounced 'soodjook') is a sausage of Armenian origin, redolent with cinnamon, cumin, garlic and chilli. It is commonly found on menus across the Middle East, the Balkans and Central Asia. On the streets of Istanbul, you will find sucuk sliced, fried and served with an egg and a slice of bread for a filling breakfast, or stuffed and baked into a pide for a delicious midday snack.

Preparation time: 5 minutes
Cooking time: 10 minutes
Serves 4
12 round sucuk slices
4 eggs

Sauté the slices of sucuk in a medium frying pan (choose one just large enough to accommodate four fried eggs nestled among the sausage slices) over medium–high heat; do not add any fat or oil. Carefully break the eggs into the pan, one by one, and cook them for about 5 minutes until just set (remember to bear in mind that the residual heat will continue to cook the eggs after you remove them from the heat source).

Note: Sucuk, a spicy cured sausage (usually beef), is available from Turkish or other Middle Eastern food shops and specialist butchers. Use another type of spicy cured sausage in its place if you can't find it.

SCRAMBLED EGGS WITH VEGETABLES
menemen

A great breakfast standard. You can add dried mint or pul biber (Aleppo pepper) or other chilli flakes when you add the tomatoes, for an extra flavour dimension.

Preparation time: 10 minutes
Cooking time: 15–20 minutes
Serves 4
2 tablespoons olive oil
1 white onion, thinly sliced
1 long green capsicum (pepper), sliced into rounds
2 tomatoes, diced
6 eggs

Heat the olive oil in a frying pan over medium heat. Add the onion, and sauté for 5 minutes, or until soft and translucent. Next, add the capsicum and tomatoes, and continue cooking for a few minutes until the vegetables have softened. Crack the eggs into the pan one at a time, season with salt and scramble by whisking together the contents of the frying pan with a fork or whisk. Allow 5–10 minutes to cook, bearing in mind that the residual heat will continue to cook the eggs once you take the pan off the heat.

TURKISH COFFEE
türk kahvesi

Coffee traditionally brings the morning meal to a close. It is a ritual that has been firmly anchored in the everyday life of Turks since its arrival in Constantinople at the beginning of the sixteenth century and the opening of the first cafés– Europe followed suit later. Until the beginning of the twentieth century, coffee was the most popular beverage across the Ottoman Empire, before the cultivation of tea in the young Turkish republic led to tea taking its place.

Preparation time: 10 minutes
2 teaspoons Turkish coffee grounds per person
granulated sugar, to taste

Mix together the coffee and sugar in a *cezve* (Turkish long-handled coffee pot). Add some cold water (allow 125 ml/4 fl oz/½ cup per demitasse or espresso cup of coffee), and mix again. Place the small pot over a low heat, and wait for the coffee to swell up. Take the *cezve* off the heat, spoon off the foam that forms on top of the coffee and use it to line the bottom of the cups. Return the *cezve* to the heat, and wait for the coffee to rise a second time: take the coffee off the heat and half-fill the cups, carefully pouring the liquid over the foam. Return the coffee to the heat: when it rises up a third time, turn off the heat, and finish serving by topping up each coffee cup until filled to the rim.

TURKISH COFFEE IS EXTRA FINELY GROUND AND IS NOTHING LIKE AN ESPRESSO GRIND: THE GROUNDS FLOW LIKE FLOUR AND ARE HEATED IN A 'CEZVE' (LITTLE COFFEE POT). DO NOT TRY TO MAKE TURKISH COFFEE WITH ANYTHING OTHER THAN COFFEE ESPECIALLY MADE FOR A CEZVE.

THE MEYHANE TABLE
MEZE AND FISH

A tradition shared by Turkey's neighbours, meze is a state of mind: that of several people gathering around a table covered with little dishes and taking the time to make the most of it. It is the spirit of Istanbul's Greek and Armenian *meyhanes* (traditional taverns), essential ingredients of this city, which for a long time brought together the peoples of Europe and the East like no other before it. There, you sample dishes with a variety of flavours, slowly drinking a bottle of rakı (the national anise-flavoured spirit, cousin to Greece's ouzo, Eastern arak and Provençal pastis), and talking about everything – for hours. You do not rush a table of meze; you savour it. Quantities are small but numerous, like the aromas. You drink – but, again, not too quickly. 'It's not the done thing to get drunk straight away. There are rules,' I've heard it said. Hors d'œuvres are served with toasted bread and olives, crudités or turşu (pickles), to nibble during the meal. They are traditionally followed by fish. Lunch becomes dinner, through sheer inertia. It is Sunday. You have time. At the table of his Agora Meyhanesı (pages 38–39) a smiling Ezel Akay concludes: 'And at the end it is always the same question: where is Turkey headed in all that?'

FROM KARAKÖY TO ÇUKURCUMA

Karaköy is the modern incarnation of Galata in Istanbul, at the
1 foot of the bridge of the same name, with its **fish market** and
balık ekmek (fish sandwiches), but it is also a neighbourhood
that is rising, changing and multiplying its new places to visit.

Behind Karaköy quay lies a host of good places, all jostling
2 for room: Go up Rihtim Caddesi and stop at *Namli Gurme*
(Rıhtım Caddesi No: 1/1) for an endless breakfast on Sunday
afternoon, or simply to sample its mercimek (lentil) köfte. It
even sells groceries. Continue along the street to Didem Şenol's
3 *Lokanta Maya (Kemankeş Caddesi No: 35/A)*, a sublime spot to
discover very fine quality Turkish cuisine (reserve for dinner).
4 Just next door, another famous address: *Karaköy Lokantası*.
There, turn left onto Galata Şarap Iskelesi Sokak, then right
(Mumhane Caddesi), go straight ahead and you will find one
of the most alluring establishments in the city – the kind
5 you go out of your way to visit every day. *Galata Simitçisi*
(Mumhane Caddesi No: 47/A) is a tiny bakery where you will want
to buy everything. All the breads. The yağlı simit is to die for.

Pera means the 'other side' in Greek: the other bank of
the Golden Horn in this case. Pera is the old Latin quarter
and the historical heart of the modern city. It boasts an
enormous concentration of restaurants and bars, where long-
standing institutions rub shoulders with new places, beside
the Istiklâl Caddesi (a pedestrian avenue), which is always
thick with people. No one really knows why the crowd is so
dense and keeps coming back – like me, for that matter.

Start your stroll with the Orient Express. The tea salon and
6 pâtisserie at *Pera Palas (Meşrutiyet Caddesi No: 52, Tepebaşı)*, built
in 1892 to satisfy the luxurious requirements of the passengers
on the Orient Express, are worth a detour just for the beauty
of the interiors (and for the mastic macarons). Next, go back
down Refik Saydam Caddesi and turn left towards Pera on
Asmalı Mescit Caddesi. The street is brimming with places at
which to stop, whether for drinks and small plates or more
7 substantial meals. *Yakup 2 (Asmalı Mescit Caddesi No: 21/B)*, a vast
old-style meyhane with wonderful acılı ezme (a spicy chopped

salad); opposite, sip a rakı accompanied by some meze – or the
8 other way around – at *Asmalı Cavit*, another institution when
it comes to taverns. At the end of the street, go up Istiklâl and,
9 opposite Galatasaray High School, visit Beyoğlu's **Balık Pazarı**, a
little market with lots of tourists, but also some good addresses:
lakerda (cured bonito) specialists, spice and offal merchants and
the pâtisserie *Sakarya Tatlıcısı (Dudu Odaları Sokak No: 3, Balık
Pazarı)*, with its kurabiye (almond shortbreads) and ayva tatlısı
(quince dessert) served with kaymak (buffalo's milk clotted
cream). Take the time to sit down with a tea, a few steps from
the frenzy of Istiklâl. Higher up, on the pedestrian thoroughfare,
10 you can also stop in at **Saray** *(No: 105, Istiklal Caddesi)*, open late
and never empty. You go in, beckoned by the window display,
and then once you are in you no longer know which sweet to
11 choose. Not far away is *Hacı Bekir (No: 83/A)*, responsible for the
invention of Turkish delight (lokum) in the eighteenth century.

Cihangir is the artists' neighbourhood: a little bohemian, a
little bourgeois and very charming with its narrow streets
lined with trees, its steep relief, its sudden views of the Golden
Horn and the Bosphorus, and its many cafés, organic food
shops and chic grocers.

Coming up from Tophane, the climb to Taksim is hard work. A
12 break in Cihangir is a must, at *Balya Organik (Defterdar Yokuşu,
Batarya Sokak, No: 16)*. It is organic, of course. On the terrace of
this café-restaurant-grocer, in the shade of the trees beside cats
taking a nap, you can enjoy a refreshing juice. Long live Cihangir!
13 Further up the street, *Van Kahvaltı Evi (Defterdar Yokuşu
No: 52/A)* sets the standard when it comes to breakfast. It is just
like the city of Van on the eastern edge of Turkey, which gives
the establishment its name – famous for its kahvaltı (breakfast)
that revived and fortified the caravan drivers passing through
on the Silk Route. Keep going up the street, turn left into
14 Firuzağa Cami Sokak and you will see *Asri Turşucu (Ağahamam
Caddesi No: 9/A)* – a compulsory destination, opened more than
a hundred years ago by the grandfather of the current owners,
and offering about 40 different pickles. It is impossible to go
past the cabbage leaves pickled in lemon juice! Sipping your
turşu (pickle) juice, keep going up towards Taksim (Defterdar
Yokuşu becomes Sıraselviler Caddesi), turn left at Bakraç Sokak,
15 then right (Oba Sokak), to find the discreet *Küçük Kurabiye
Dükkani*, at the end of a little street, a rather hidden spot
for such very good home-made kurabiye.

PICKLES
turşu

In the neighbourhood of Çukurcuma, among the antiques stores and funny little bric-a-brac shops, you cannot miss the window display of **Asri Turşucu**. Dozens of large glass jars are stacked from the floor to (almost) the ceiling, filled with pickled vegetables and sealed with little gingham caps in a rainbow of colours. Irresistible. Each summer the shop closes to renew its stocks. The business first opened in 1913 and moved to the neighbourhood in 1938. The third generation is now at the helm, and I swear by their lemon pickle. It is so good you can even drink the juice. My recipe uses vinegar.

Preparation time: 5 minutes
Resting time: 10 days before opening
250 ml (9 fl oz/1 cup) white vinegar
1 tablespoon sweet paprika
100 g (3½ oz) pickling salt
selection of raw vegetables (such as carrot sticks, baby cucumbers,
capsicums (peppers), mild chillies, whole beetroot (beets),
shredded cabbage, garlic, even chickpeas...)

Stir the vinegar, paprika and salt into 1 litre (35 fl oz/4 cups) water; continue stirring until the salt has completely dissolved. Firmly pack the vegetables into a sterilised glass jar with a tight-fitting lid, allowing room at the top to cover the vegetables with the pickling liquid (you may need more than one jar depending on its size and the size and shape of your vegetables). Pour in the pickling liquid until the vegetables are well covered. Seal the jar so that it is airtight, and store in a cool, dark place for 10 days or so before opening, to allow the vegetables to pickle evenly and the flavour to develop. The pickles will keep for up to a week if stored in the refrigerator once the seal is broken. Serve as an hors d'œuvre or as part of a meze table.

EGGPLANT PURÉE
közde patlıcan

This eggplant dish with a hint of smokiness can be served with crusty bread, and is especially good with toasted bread. To cook the eggplants (you can use this technique for capsicums and chestnuts too), try to find a *közmatik*. This is a sort of frying pan with holes in it that is specially designed for cooking on coals, and is how the dish gets its name (*közde* means 'over coals').

Preparation time: 10 minutes
Cooking time: 30 minutes
Serves 4
2 eggplants (aubergines)
½ onion, very finely chopped
1 very ripe tomato, very finely diced
juice of 1 small lemon
1 generous tablespoon extra virgin olive oil
a few flat-leaf (Italian) parsley sprigs, chopped

Prick the eggplants in several places with a fork, then place them on the heat – on a barbecue, in a *közmatik* or directly over a gas flame; otherwise put them under a hot grill (broiler) – turning them over regularly, for between 20 and 30 minutes, depending on their size. Once the skin of the eggplants has blackened and blistered all over, and the flesh is very tender (really melting), carefully scrape out the flesh with a spoon. Discard any seeds and the skin, and mash the flesh with a fork. Combine the eggplant purée, onion, tomato and lemon juice in a bowl. Season with salt, stir in the olive oil and scatter over the parsley. Serve cold.

ANTAKYA SPICY PURÉE
ekşili Antakya

The city of Antakya, on the Syrian border, is famous for its food, and Antakya is where this recipe originates. This spicy little dip is on the menu of the **Agora Meyhanesi 1890** (see pages 38–39) in the neighbourhood of Balat, on the bank of the Golden Horn.

Preparation time: 10 minutes
Soaking time: 30 minutes
Serves 4

100 g (3½ oz) sun-dried tomatoes (not those stored in oil), finely chopped
a few long dried red chillies (optional, for those who like it burning hot), finely chopped
boiling water
100 ml (3½ fl oz) extra virgin olive oil, plus extra for drizzling
2 large tablespoons tatlı biber salçası (mild Turkish chilli paste) (see note)
30 g (1 oz/¼ cup) coarsely ground walnuts
2 tablespoons pomegranate molasses (available from Turkish or other Middle Eastern food shops, some supermarkets and online)

Put the sun-dried tomatoes and chillies (if using) in a small bowl. Pour over boiling water to cover, drizzle with a little olive oil and leave to soak for 30 minutes; drain. Put the soaked tomatoes (and chillies) in a food processor with the biber salçası, ground walnuts, pomegranate molasses and the 100 ml (3½ fl oz) olive oil. Season with salt, and pulse to form a rough paste. Alternatively, pound together using a mortar and pestle. Serve with slices of dry lightly toasted bread.

Note: Biber salçası, a thick, red paste, is widely used in Turkish cooking. Made from chillies or capsicums (peppers), or both, from which the stems and seeds have been removed, before being dried in the sun, it comes in two basic variations: (very) hot (acı biber salçası) or mild (tatlı biber salçası). You can buy it from Turkish or other Middle Eastern food shops.

WARNING: THIS IS HOT! ESPECIALLY IF YOU ADD A FEW DRIED CHILLIES. DO SO ACCORDING TO YOUR TASTES AND HEAT TOLERANCE.

'SPICY PASTE'
acılı ezme

Another very common version of a rather spicy meze is ezme, a very, very finely chopped salad. The smoother paste version of this dish calls for each ingredient to be cut into very small pieces. The pul biber found in this recipe, often used to season dishes in Turkey, is made from chillies that have had their stems and seeds removed, before being sun-dried, then crushed. For a variation, try piment d'Espelette (Espelette pepper), which is produced in the Basque region of France, in place of the pul biber.

Preparation time: 45 minutes
Resting time: 1 hour
Serves 4
1 red onion, finely diced
1 teaspoon sumac
½ teaspoon salt
2 large tomatoes, blanched, peeled, seeded and diced
1 long green capsicum (pepper), seeded and diced
1 green chilli, seeded and diced
2 garlic cloves, crushed
2 large handfuls flat-leaf (Italian) parsley, very finely chopped
a few mint sprigs, very finely chopped
1 tablespoon tatlı biber salçası (mild Turkish chilli paste)
    (see note on page 34)
1 tablespoon pomegranate molasses (available from Turkish or other
    Middle Eastern food shops, some supermarkets and online)
pul biber (Aleppo pepper) or other chilli flakes (see note)
juice of ½ lemon
60 ml (2 fl oz/¼ cup) extra virgin olive oil
1 handful chopped walnuts, to serve

Combine the onion, sumac and salt in a medium bowl. Add the tomatoes, capsicum, green chilli, garlic and herbs. In another, small bowl, mix together the chilli paste, pomegranate molasses, a pinch of chilli flakes, a little freshly ground black pepper, the lemon juice and olive oil. Add to the contents of the first bowl, and stir through. Leave to rest in the refrigerator for 1 hour. Scatter over the walnuts, and serve with slices of dry toasted bread.

Note: Pul biber is the Turkish term for chilli flakes. Also known as Aleppo pepper, its sweetness and heat may vary. More moist than other chilli flakes, it is made from semi-dried and deseeded chillies. Look for it in Turkish or other Middle Eastern food shops, or substitute with other chilli flakes to taste.

In 2014 Ezel Akay opened Agora Meyhanese 1890 in a building that had housed an old meyhane (tavern) dating from 1890. That tavern had closed in the early 2000s, and the new name reflects the establishment's beginnings. Ezel did this to restore the heartbeat of Balat, the old Jewish quarter, with its lively working class, and also to continue the culture of the meyhane, with its Greek and Armenian dishes and the 'rakı table'. People go to Ezel's place to talk and to share dishes among friends. You have a taste of everything, drink slowly, one more glass, one more meze, and it goes on and on, and you feel good. 'And at the end, we're all one big family!' In his other life, Ezel is a film director. He has travelled a lot and describes himself as 'from nowhere and therefore from everywhere.' He sees cooking in the same way as he shoots his films: 'It's like telling a story. The ingredients become words. Put together, they become stories. It's good to tell stories.' And you keep listening – and have another glass of rakı.

EZEL'S RECIPES

Ekşili Antakya (Antakya spicy purée, page 34), lakerda (cured bonito, page 54), skordalia (garlic and walnut purée, page 56), *Agora* kalamar (Agora squid with sauce, page 66), levrek marine (marinated sea bass, page 72).

ADDRESS

Agora Meyhanesi 1890, Mürselpaşa Caddesi No: 185, Ayvansaray, Fatih

EZEL AKAY

Restaurateur and film director,
Agora Meyhanesi 1890 (Balat)

CHOPPED SALAD WITH WALNUTS
gavurdağı salatası

A salad made from ingredients typical of Turkish cuisine: tomatoes, long capsicums, walnuts, spring onions, lemon, olive oil… The long capsicum is the most common variety found in Turkey. It is smaller than the bell capsicum, and sweeter as well.

Preparation time: 15 minutes
Serves 4
4 tomatoes, diced
4 small Lebanese (short) cucumbers (or 1 large), diced
4 long green capsicums (peppers) (or 1 very large), seeded
    and diced
3 small bulb spring onions (scallions), finely chopped
1 handful flat-leaf (Italian) parsley, finely chopped
100 g (3½ oz/generous ¾ cup) roughly chopped walnuts
juice of 1 lemon
80 ml (2½ fl oz/⅓ cup) extra virgin olive oil

Put all the ingredients in a medium bowl, stirring through gently. Season with salt.

YOGHURT WITH CUCUMBER
cacık

Cacık (pronounced 'djadjek') is the twin of the Greek tzatziki. Sometimes more liquid-y in Turkey than variations found in neighbouring countries, it can also be flavoured with dried mint or finely chopped dill. A classic of the meze table, cacık wis also served with meat dishes or kebabs.

Preparation time: 5 minutes
Resting time: 30 minutes
Serves 4
200 g (7 oz) Lebanese (short) cucumbers
1 or 2 garlic cloves
300 g (10½ oz/generous 1 cup) Turkish or Greek-style yoghurt
dried or finely chopped herbs (such as dill or mint) (optional)
extra virgin olive oil

Peel the cucumber if you like, then grate the flesh into a large bowl. Salt it and leave to stand for 30 minutes, to disgorge any liquid. Drain well. Using a mortar and pestle, crush the garlic with some salt. Mix it into the yoghurt – into just a tablespoon of yoghurt first, then add the rest of the yoghurt, so that the garlic mixes through evenly. Add the cucumber and a few pinches of herbs (if using), stir through, then drizzle with olive oil. Serve at room temperature.

PARSLEY SALAD
maydanoz salatası

Sumac comes from the dried and crushed fruits of a shrub or small tree (Rhus coriaria), and is a widely used spice in Middle Eastern and Mediterranean cuisine. With its acidic taste, it is a good substitute for lemon as a seasoning.

Preparation time: 10 minutes
Serves 4
60 ml (2 fl oz/¼ cup) extra virgin olive oil
2 tablespoons sumac molasses or pomegranate molasses (see note)
300 g (10½ oz/2 large bunches) flat-leaf (Italian) parsley, stalks removed
2 handfuls roughly chopped walnuts (about 80 g/2¾ oz/⅔ cup)
2 teaspoons sumac

Put the olive oil and molasses in a small bowl. Season with salt to taste, and stir to combine. Dress the parsley with this sauce, then add the walnuts and ground sumac.

Note: Sumac molasses is similar to pomegranate molasses, with the same tart–sweet balance in its flavour profile, and is made from the fruits of the same shrub as dried sumac. Look for it at Turkish or other Middle Eastern food shops, specialist or gourmet grocers and good delicatessens.

CHICKPEA POCKETS
topik

An Armenian meze, these chickpea pockets are better if made the day before eating, so that the dish has time to develop all its flavours. Thank you to Annie Yazician, who opened up her magnificent recipe notebook for me.

Preparation time: 40 minutes
Soaking time (chickpeas): overnight
Resting time: at least 4 hours
Cooking time: 1 hour 30 minutes
Serves 10–12 (4 pockets)
450 g (1 lb/2¼ cups) dried chickpeas (about 1 kg/2 lb 4 oz/6¼ cups cooked)
2 large all-purpose potatoes (such as desiree)
1.5 kg (3 lb 5 oz) mild, sweet onions (such as Cévennes), finely chopped
75 g (2¾ oz/½ cup) pine nuts
75 g (2¾ oz/½ cup) currants
1 tablespoon ground cinnamon
1 teaspoon ground allspice
2 generous tablespoons tahini

The day before cooking, soak the chickpeas in plenty of cold water. The next day, rinse the chickpeas in a colander. Tip into a large saucepan, cover well with fresh cold water and bring to the boil. Simmer for 1½ hours, or until tender. Drain, then remove the loosened skins; set aside. Peel, halve and boil the potatoes until tender; drain and set aside. Meanwhile, in a separate pan, simmer the onions in 1 litre (35 fl oz/4 cups) water, covered, for 45 minutes. Remove to a sieve using a slotted spoon (keep the liquid). Squeeze out any excess liquid, first by hand, then by sitting a plate on top. Once the onions have cooled, combine with the pine nuts, currants, cinnamon, allspice and tahini. Season with salt. Rinse and drain the cooked chickpeas, then put through a food mill with the potatoes, or crush with a fork. Divide the mixture into four balls. Place a ball on a large rectangle of plastic wrap, gently flatten by hand, cover with another sheet of plastic wrap and roll out to a 20 cm (8 inch) square. Brush with the reserved onion cooking liquid, and place a quarter of the onion mixture in the middle. Fold over one corner, then the opposite corner of the square with the help of the plastic wrap (so you don't break the fragile dough); do the same with the other two corners. Gently press the four corners with your fingers to seal completely. Make three more topik in the same way. Wrap each little packet in plastic wrap and set aside in the refrigerator for several hours, or even a day or two. To serve, remove the plastic and turn the topik over so you don't see the 'join'.

DIDEM'S BROAD BEANS
Didem'in baklası

A recipe from Didem Şenol, the chef at **Lokanta Maya** in Karaköy and **Gram** in Beyoğlu and Sarıyer (see pages 178–179). An excellent way of preparing fresh broad beans – namely whole, including the pods.

Preparation time: 15 minutes
Cooking time: 10 minutes
Serves 4
800 g (1 lb 12 oz) fresh broad beans in their pods
8 sandwich bread slices
50 g (1¾ oz) Turkish or Greek-style yoghurt
35 ml (1¼ fl oz) white vinegar
75 g (2¾ oz/⅔ cup) walnuts
1 small handful dill

Preheat the oven to 150°C (300°F). Arrange the bread in a single layer on a baking tray, and dry in the oven for 10 minutes. Meanwhile, bring plenty of water to the boil in a large saucepan. Add the whole broad beans, cook for 5–10 minutes, then rinse in cold water. Using a blender or food processor, pulse the dried bread with the rest of the ingredients, except the broad beans, to make a chunky sauce. Season with salt and freshly ground black pepper. Combine the sauce with the broad beans, and serve cold.

SAMPHIRE SALAD WITH ALMONDS

bademli deniz börülcesi salatası

Samphire grows on the coast and in coastal marshes – hence its salty flavour – and makes a very, very good salad. It is commonly found on the menu of meyhanes (taverns), and is sold fresh at good fishmongers and specialist food shops, or pickled at specialist grocery shops and delicatessens.

Preparation time: 15 minutes
Serves 4

400 g (14 oz) fresh or pickled samphire
zest of 2 lemons, cut into fine strips or grated
zest of 1 orange, cut into fine strips or grated
100 g (3½ oz/⅔ cup) roughly chopped
**   blanched almonds**
90 ml (3 fl oz) extra virgin olive oil
2 tablespoons lemon juice
2 garlic cloves, crushed

Rinse the fresh samphire under cold running water, and remove any tough stems or roots. Break up any larger pieces into smaller stems. Next, blanch the fresh samphire in boiling water for 10 minutes; refresh under cold water. (If you are using pickled samphire, just rinse it well.) Drain the samphire, and put in a bowl. Add the lemon and orange zests and the almonds. Make the vinaigrette by whisking together the olive oil, lemon juice and crushed garlic, and use to dress the salad.

GARLIC YOGHURT
haydari

A dish that's simple, quick and essential to the meze table. Serve with slices of toasted bread.

Preparation time: 5 minutes
Serves 4
2 garlic cloves
200 g (7 oz/¾ cup) Turkish or Greek-style yoghurt (see note)
1 generous tablespoon dried mint
extra virgin olive oil (optional)

Crush the garlic with some salt using a mortar and pestle. Mix into 1 tablespoon of the yoghurt in a bowl, before adding the rest of the yoghurt, so that the garlic mixes through evenly. Sprinkle over the dried mint, and drizzle with a little olive oil (if using).

Note: Turkish or Greek-style yoghurt is thicker, creamier and richer than the 'normal' tub of plain yoghurt; Turkish yoghurt is available from Turkish or other Middle Eastern food shops or larger supermarkets.

EGGPLANT WITH YOGHURT
yoğurtlu patlıcan

The eggplant is the vegetable emblem of Turkish food. Prepared every which way – as a salad, purée, fried – it develops an incomparable smoky flavour when grilled over a flame. It mellows even more when combined with yoghurt. Choose smaller, sweeter eggplants (and avoid the huge, spongy ones, which do not turn meltingly soft).

Preparation time: 10 minutes
Cooking time: 30 minutes
Serves 4
2 eggplants (aubergines)
2 long green capsicums (peppers)
1 garlic clove
½ teaspoon salt
100 g (3½ oz) Turkish or Greek-style yoghurt
1 generous tablespoon extra virgin olive oil

Prick the eggplants and capsicums in several places with a fork, then place them on the heat on a barbecue, in a *közmatik* (see page 32) or directly over a gas flame; otherwise put them under a hot grill (broiler) – turning them over regularly, for between 20 and 30 minutes, depending on their size. (The capsicums will take less time, being smaller.) The flesh needs to be meltingly soft. Crush the garlic with the salt using a mortar and pestle. Mix it with 1 tablespoon of the yoghurt in a bowl, before adding the rest of the yoghurt, so that the garlic mixes through evenly. Carefully peel the eggplants and capsicums (discard the skin), using a pair of tongs to hold the vegetables if they are too hot. Remove and discard the seeds and membranes from the capsicums. Mash the eggplant and capsicum flesh with a fork, and combine with the yoghurt. Drizzle with the olive oil, and serve cold with slices of dry toasted bread.

CURED BONITO
lakerda

'Cooked' in salt and served with red onion rings, bonito becomes a meze to die for. Discover it at **Balık Pazarı** (the fish market) in Beyoğlu (see page 27).

Preparation time: 1 hour
Curing time: 15–20 days
Desalting time: 12 hours
**1 fresh bonito, gutted and cleaned
coarse salt
olive oil**

Remove the head and tail of the fish, then cut into (vertical) slices 7–8 cm (2¾–3¼ inches) wide, leaving the skin on. Soak the slices of fish in a large bowl of cold water for 1 hour, to draw out the blood, then rinse them several times to remove all traces. Place the slices of bonito in a large glass dish with a generous layer of salt on the bottom, making sure that they fit quite snugly, then cover completely with another generous layer of salt. Next, cover the dish tightly with plastic wrap, and set a plate or similar on top to weigh it down and help to prevent air getting to the fish. Transfer to the refrigerator to cure. Pour off the liquid that is drawn out of the fish on a regular basis, and monitor the progress of the curing process. After 15–20 days (depending on the size of the fish), the salt will have done its work – no more liquid will disgorge from the fish and the flesh will be tender. Rinse the fish under cold running water, then submerge it in fresh cold water for half a day. Remove and discard the skin, cut each slice into smaller pieces and keep in an airtight jar, well covered with olive oil. The lakerda will keep for one month in the oil.

BONITO IS AN OILY FISH FROM THE SAME FAMILY AS TUNA. IT SWIMS IN THE MEDITERRANEAN AND BLACK SEAS - IN OTHER WORDS, ALL AROUND ISTANBUL.

GARLIC AND WALNUT PURÉE
skordalia

A meze with Greek origins, this version is courtesy of Ezel Akav at the **Agora Meyhanesi 1890** (see pages 38–39). New or green garlic is available in late spring and at the beginning of summer (and is a particular find at farmers' and growers' markets), and has a milder flavour than dried garlic.

Preparation time: 15 minutes
Serves 4
100 g (3½ oz) new (fresh green or spring) garlic
100 g (3½ oz/generous ¾ cup) roughly chopped walnuts
extra virgin olive oil

Peel the garlic, then crush it with a little salt using a mortar and pestle, or whiz into a paste in a food processor. Combine the garlic paste with the chopped walnuts. Add a drizzle of olive oil. Serve with slices of dry toasted bread.

BROAD BEAN PURÉE
fava

You can find dried broad beans, with or without their skins, in Turkish, other Middle Eastern and Mediterranean food shops. If you use skinless broad beans, allow 150 g (5½ oz).

Preparation time: 15 minutes
Soaking time (broad beans): overnight
Cooking time: 30 minutes
Serves 4
200 g (7 oz) dried broad beans
60 ml (2 fl oz/¼ cup) olive oil, plus extra as needed
1 small onion, finely diced
1 carrot, finely diced
1 or 2 garlic cloves, finely chopped
juice of 1 lemon
extra virgin olive oil

The day before cooking, soak the broad beans in a large bowl of cold water. The next day, drain and rinse the beans in a colander under cold running water, before cooking for 5 minutes in a saucepan of boiling water. Drain once again, and remove the loosened skins; set aside. Heat the 60 ml (2 fl oz/¼ cup) olive oil in a large frying pan over medium heat. Add the onion, carrot and garlic, and sauté for 5 minutes or so until the onion is soft and translucent. Tip the beans into the pan, and stir through. Season with salt, cover and continue cooking over medium heat for a further 25 minutes, or until the beans are very tender and starting to fall apart. Once cooked, purée the vegetables in a blender or food processor (adding a little extra olive oil to smooth out the purée). Allow the purée to cool, then stir through the lemon juice and a drizzle of extra virgin olive oil. Serve cold.

PURSLANE SALAD WITH YOGHURT

yoğurtlu semizotu salatası

A little plant with round leaves, purslane can be found in spring and summer at good greengrocers. You can dress it with yoghurt, or with olive oil and sumac, with a dash of pomegranate molasses.

Preparation time: 10 minutes
Serves 4
2 garlic cloves
80 g (2¾ oz) Turkish or Greek-style yoghurt
a little iced water (if needed)
100 g (3½ oz) purslane, washed and leaves picked
extra virgin olive oil
pul biber (Aleppo pepper) or other chilli flakes

To make the yoghurt sauce, crush the garlic with some salt using a mortar and pestle. Add it to a tablespoon of the yoghurt in a bowl, before adding the rest of the yoghurt, so that the garlic mixes through evenly. Beat the yoghurt mixture, adding a little iced water if the yoghurt is too thick, to make a creamy sauce. Dress the purslane with a drizzle of olive oil and the yoghurt sauce. Sprinkle with a pinch of chilli flakes, and serve cold.

PURSLANE! THERE IS NOTHING BETTER FOR MAKING A TASTY SALAD.

TURKISH TABOULEH
Hande's kısır

Kısır is Turkish tabouleh, traditionally made from burghul, tomatoes, capsicums (peppers) and fresh herbs. Hande Bozdoğan, the lovely founder of the Istanbul Culinary Institute (see pages 164–165), gave me her version, which is both sweet (from the beetroot) and sour (from the pomegranate molasses and balsamic vinegar). The pomegranate molasses used to dress this salad is very different from pomegranate juice, and far more like a thick vinegar. Do not overlook it because it has a unique sweet–sour flavour.

Preparation time: 15 minutes
Cooking time: 10 minutes
Serves 4
150 g (5½ oz) fine burghul (bulgur)
2 beetroot (beets), trimmed, cooked and peeled (see note below)
extra virgin olive oil
½ teaspoon balsamic vinegar
2 bulb spring onions (scallions), finely chopped
3 or 4 flat-leaf (Italian) parsley sprigs, finely chopped
2 or 3 fresh thyme sprigs, leaves picked and finely chopped
pul biber (Aleppo pepper) or other chilli flakes
1 generous teaspoon pomegranate molasses (available from Turkish or other Middle Eastern food shops, some supermarkets and online)

Bring 300 ml (10½ fl oz) water to the boil in a saucepan, and add the burghul. Cover and cook over low heat for about 10 minutes, then set aside. Purée one of the beetroot in a blender or food processor with a little olive oil and the balsamic vinegar. Dice the other beetroot, and add the diced beetroot and the purée to the burghul. Next, add the spring onions, parsley, thyme, a pinch of chilli flakes and a good pinch of salt. Stir through, then add the pomegranate molasses and a little more olive oil. Stir through again, and serve cold.

Note: To cook beetroot, wrap them in foil and roast in a preheated oven at 200°C (400°F) for 1–1½ hours. (Insert a knife into the flesh to check whether they are done: they are cooked when they are tender and the flesh is easily pierced.) Peel once they are cool enough to handle.

BLACK-EYED PEA SALAD
kuru börülce salatasi

The black-eyed pea is a small pale dried bean tattooed with a black circle (hence its name). You can find this legume in Turkish or other Middle Eastern food shops if your local supermarket or grocer does not have them on the shelf.

Preparation time: 10 minutes
Cooking time: 40 minutes
Serves 4
200 g (7 oz/1 cup) dried black-eyed peas, picked over and rinsed
2 bulb spring onions (scallions), very thinly sliced
2 large tomatoes, diced
60 ml (2 fl oz/¼ cup) extra virgin olive oil
juice of ½ lemon
1 large handful flat-leaf (Italian) parsley, chopped

Put the black-eyed peas in a large saucepan. Cover with plenty of cold water, and bring to the boil. Reduce the heat to a simmer, and cook for 40 minutes, skimming off any grey scum that rises to the surface, or until the peas are tender but not mushy. Meanwhile, mix together the spring onions and tomatoes in a large bowl. Once the black-eyed peas are cooked, drain and rinse under cold running water. Drain again, then add to the tomato mixture. Stir through gently. Drizzle with the olive oil and lemon juice, and sprinkle with the parsley.

AGORA SQUID
WITH SAUCE
Agora kalamar

Fish sauce was not originally imported from afar to Turkey, but made instead by the Greeks. Its manufacture, similar to that of the Classical Roman garum, has fallen away. This is a recipe from the **Agora Meyhanesi** in Balat (see pages 38–39). Perhaps fish sauce will be reborn at the **Agora**, which aims to revive the customary know-how and traditions of the meyhanes, all in-house.

Preparation time: 5 minutes
Resting time: 8 hours
Cooking time: 10 minutes
Serves 4
MARINADE
500 g (1 lb 2 oz) squid tubes
200 ml (7 fl oz) olive oil
1 large onion, grated
2 tablespoons dijon mustard
1 tablespoon fish sauce (such as nuoc mam)
1 tablespoon dried oregano
SAUCE
300 g (10½ oz) crème fraîche
1 garlic clove, grated
100 ml (3½ fl oz) fish sauce (such as nuoc mam)
20 g (¾ oz) butter, melted
1 tablespoon rice starch

To clean the squid, gently pull the tentacles away from the tube (the intestines should come away at the same time). Remove the intestines from the tentacles by cutting under the eyes, then remove the beak if it remains in the centre of the tentacles by using your fingers to push up the centre. Pull away the quill (the transparent cartilage) from inside the body and remove. Remove and discard any white membrane. Under cold running water, pull the skin away from the hood. Cut into rings, and put in a glass or ceramic dish. Mix together the olive oil, onion, fish sauce and oregano. Pour over the squid, cover with plastic wrap and marinate in the refrigerator for 8 hours. Make the sauce several hours in advance. Combine the crème fraîche and garlic. Gently mix in the fish sauce, 60 ml (2 fl oz/¼ cup) water, the melted butter and rice starch (blended into a little water to make a paste). Set aside to chill; bring to room temperature not long before cooking the squid. Drain the squid, and cook in a chargrill pan over medium–high heat for about 10 minutes. Serve with the sauce.

MUSSEL FRITTERS
midye tava

Simple and very good, these morsels are ideal for enjoying with a glass of rakı, as a starter or appetiser, or as part of a crowd of meze.

Preparation time: 15 minutes
Cooking time: 15 minutes
Serves 4
100 g (3½ oz/⅔ cup) self-raising flour
150 ml (5 fl oz) beer
oil for deep-frying (such as olive oil or peanut/groundnut oil)
200 g (7 oz) shelled mussels (if using frozen mussels, drop them into a saucepan of boiling water for 2 minutes first)
SAUCE
100 g (3½ oz/⅔ cup) pine nuts and/or walnuts, ground in a food processor
red wine vinegar
3 sandwich bread slices, crusts removed, soaked in water and gently squeezed dry
2 garlic cloves

Combine the flour and beer to make a batter, and season with salt. Heat enough oil for deep-frying in a small heavy-based saucepan over medium heat until it reaches 180°C (350°F), or until a cube of bread dropped into the oil turns golden brown within 15 seconds. Using a long, thin skewer, dip the mussels into the batter one by one, and deep-fry in the hot oil for 2 minutes, or just as long as it takes the batter to become golden brown all over. Leave to drain on a plate lined with paper towel; keep warm. To make the sauce, grind the nuts using a mortar and pestle, or in a food processor. Mix with a little vinegar in a small bowl, then add the soaked bread. Whisk to combine. Crush the garlic with a little salt, and add to the sauce. Continue whisking, adding a little more vinegar if needed, until you have a sauce that is the consistency of mayonnaise. Serve the fritters warm, with the bread sauce for dipping.

DIP THE LITTLE MUSSEL FRITTERS IN THE SAUCE AND *AFIYET OLSUN*¹

¹OR, BON APPÉTIT!

FRIED ANCHOVIES
hamsi tava

There are times when simple is best – and this
is one of them. Serve with lemon wedges for
squeezing over, a fresh salad and onion rings.

Preparation time: 5 minutes
Cooking time: 20 minutes
Serves 4
400 g (14 oz) fresh anchovies, scaled and gutted
plain (all-purpose) flour
3 tablespoons olive oil for pan-frying, plus extra as needed

Rinse the anchovies and pat dry with paper towel. Season with salt.
Put some flour on a plate, and dredge the anchovies on both sides in
the flour, carefully shaking off any excess. Heat the 3 tablespoons olive oil
in a large frying pan over medium heat. Working in batches so that you
do not overcrowd the pan, pan-fry the anchovies for a few minutes on
each side, depending on the size of the fish; be careful not to overcook
(and top up with oil as needed as you cook). Serve immediately.

MARINATED SEA BASS
levrek marine

A Mediterranean meze from the **Agora Meyhanesi 1890** (see pages 38–39) that is as fresh and good as it is quick to make. In this dish it is the lemon juice that gently cooks the fish.

Preparation time: 10 minutes
Resting time: 8 hours
Serves 4
300 g (10½ oz) sea bass or barramundi fillets
juice of 1½ large lemons, separated
extra virgin olive oil
a few flat-leaf (Italian) parsley sprigs
a few dill sprigs
chopped red chilli (optional)

Rinse the fillets and pat dry with paper towel. Put the fish in a glass or ceramic dish or bowl just large enough to hold the fillets snugly. Drizzle over the juice of 1 lemon. Leave to marinate in the refrigerator for at least 8 hours. Remove the fish from the marinade, and dress with the remaining lemon juice. Season with a little salt, then add a good drizzle of olive oil and scatter over the parsley, dill and a little chilli (if using).

⊙CT⊙PUS SALAD
ahtapot salatası

Choose smaller octopus over larger ones because they will be more tender. To tenderise the flesh even further, freeze the octopus for 24 hours after gutting and cleaning; the cooking time will be noticeably shorter.

Preparation time: 20 minutes
Cooking time: at least 30 minutes
Serves 4
500 g (1 lb 2 oz) octopus
2 long red capsicums (peppers),
seeded and cut into strips
2 long green capsicums (peppers),
seeded and diced
2 tablespoons dill or oregano leaves
juice of ½ lemon
extra virgin olive oil

Prepare the octopus the day before cooking. Using a small knife, carefully cut between the head and tentacles of the octopus, just below the eyes. Grasp the body of the octopus and push the beak out and up through the centre of the tentacles with your finger. Cut the eyes from the head of the octopus by slicing a small disc off with a sharp knife. Discard the eye section. To clean the octopus head, carefully slit through one side, avoiding the ink sac, and scrape out any guts from inside. Rinse under running water to remove any remaining grit. Now place them in the freezer for 24 hours to tenderise. The next day, drop the octopus into a saucepan of boiling water and cook for at least 30 minutes (depending on their size), until the flesh is quite tender. Cut the tentacles and head into short lengths, and combine with the capsicums and dill in a bowl. Dress with the lemon juice and a drizzle of olive oil, and season with salt. Serve chilled, with a salad of crisp greens if liked.

SEA BASS STEW

levrek güveç

Güveç – the word refers to a (closed) earthenware dish in which a hodgepodge of ingredients are cooked together in the oven. In the absence of one of these, you can use another type of casserole or an ovenproof dish covered with foil. This sea bass güveç, sampled at the cooking school restaurant of Kadir Has University (see page 165), is the creation of chef Bugra. Thanks, chef.

Preparation time: 20 minutes
Cooking time: 35 minutes
Serves 4

80 ml (2½ fl oz/⅓ cup) olive oil
4 small onions, very thinly sliced
3 tomatoes, finely chopped
3 tablespoons pitted olives, thinly sliced
1 tablespoon Worcestershire sauce
2 teaspoons fish sauce (such as nuoc mam)
pinch of caster (superfine) sugar
4 garlic cloves, finely chopped
1 small handful flat-leaf (Italian) parsley, chopped
grated zest of 1 lemon
4 sea bass or bonito or barramundi fillets
pul biber (Aleppo pepper) or other chilli flakes

Preheat the oven to 180°C (350°F). Heat the olive oil in a heavy-based frying pan over medium heat. Add the onions and sauté for about 15 minutes until they start to caramelise. Tip in the tomatoes and olives, and continue to cook, stirring, for a further 3 minutes. Add the Worcestershire sauce, fish sauce and sugar, and season with salt. Arrange a layer of the onion-tomato-olive mixture in the bottom of a large earthenware casserole or ovenproof dish (or four small individual ovenproof dishes). Next, add a little of the garlic, parsley and lemon zest, and season with salt. Place the fish fillets on top, then add another layer using the remaining garlic, parsley and lemon zest. Cover with a final layer of the onion-tomato-olive mixture, and sprinkle with chilli flakes to taste. Now cover the dish, and bake in the oven for 15 minutes, uncovering the dish 2 minutes before the end of the cooking time. Serve hot with a rice pilav (see page 120).

MUSSEL PILAKI
midye pilaki

A *pilaki* is a bit like a Turkish version of pot-au-feu: an assortment of vegetables (carrots, tomatoes, potatoes, others ...) simmered with your choice of meat or fish.

Preparation time: 15 minutes
Cooking time: 20 minutes
Serves 4
60 ml (2 fl oz/¼ cup) sunflower oil
2 all-purpose potatoes (such as desiree), peeled and diced
1 carrot, diced
2 garlic cloves
300 g (10½ oz) shelled mussels
250 g (9 oz/1 cup) tinned crushed tomatoes
1 small handful flat-leaf (Italian) parsley, chopped

Heat the sunflower oil in a large frying pan over medium–high heat. Add the potatoes, carrot and garlic, and sauté for 2 minutes. Next, add the crushed tomatoes and 150 ml (5 fl oz) water, cover and cook for about 10 minutes. When the vegetables are still slightly al dente, add the mussels and season with salt. Continue cooking for a further 5 minutes, covered. Sprinkle over the parsley just before serving.

LOKANTA, KÖFTECI, KEBABCI

SOUPS, MEATS AND RICE

Whether humble cafeterias or chic restaurants, lokanta serve traditional Turkish dishes. Other institutions – kebabci, ocakbaşi and köfteci – are temples of meat. Meat is especially enjoyed in Turkey: cooked or raw, grilled of course, in the form of köfte (meatballs), in stews, in a quick sandwich on the run, in a börek or on a pizza – not to mention offal and tripe. There is an abundance of choice. Tradition also dictates that a meal begins with a soup and ends with pilav (rice). Firmly rooted in Ottoman cuisine, soups and rice remain dishes shared all across Turkey – from north to south, coast to inland – by everyone, rich or poor.

Fetih Paşa Korusu

Limanı

Paşa

Sok.

Mihrimah Camii

Üsküdar Ferry Terminal

Servilik Caddesi

Cumhuriyet

Caddesi

Bülbül Deresi Mezarlığı

M Üsküdar

Yeni Valide Camii

Pak Caddesi

Mumhane Sok.

Aşçı Hanım Sok.

Uncalar Cad.

Ali Efendi

Caddesi

ÜSKÜDAR

Şair Ruhi Sok.

Caddesi

Açık Türbe Sokak

Doğancılar

Davutoğlu Sok.

Toptaşı

Çavuşdere

Caddesi

İskele

Daye Kadın

THE ASIAN SIDE

Istanbul has the unique status in the world of being a city that spans two continents. The Asian side has fewer tourists than the European side, fewer people as well, but is no less lively and active. The two sides are linked by two long bridges suspended above the Bosphorus, a subway line and a constant back-and-forth of water buses. Sailing on the strait, you gain an even better sense of the beauty and scale of the city. It is like taking a step back and seeing the overall picture. There are rows of palaces, kiosks, pavilions and mosques by the water: Dolmabahçe, Çırağan and the Ortaköy Mosque on the European side; Beylerbeyi Sarayı the Asian. All around is the outline of the city's hills, with their domes, minarets, towers and countless apartment blocks, and it is perhaps this vast horizon that is the most staggering sight. Moving up the eastern bank, the magnificent painted-wood Ottoman houses (the yalı) look like a perfect mixture of Europe and Asia.

1 A couple of steps from the quay of Üsküdar, a large and conservative Istanbul neighbourhood, behind the Mihrimah mosque, is **Bingöl Bal Pazarı** (*Selmanağa Çeşme Sokak No: 1, Üsküdar*), a tiny honey shop that sells everything related to the beehive (honey, pollen, wax) and has its own unique house blends. Try its special honey-royal jelly-spice blend. Then take

2 Selmanipak Caddesi to have lunch at **Kanaat Lokantası** (*Selmanipak Caddesi No: 9*), a venerable institution of Turkish gastronomy on the Asian side. Further still up the street,

3 turn right onto Atlas Sokak, then left, and stop at **Aytekin Erol** (*Atlas Sokak No: 21, Balıkçılar Çarşısı*). Its production of Turkish delight has been handed down from father to son. You will find all the flavours and colours of creation here (try the kaymak ones!), but also other sweet treats and candies (melon-flavoured), including all kinds of helva (including with almond paste), and all made according to traditional methods. Aytekin Erol's father opened the Üsküdar shop in 1945. His grandfather before him began in Kadıköy.

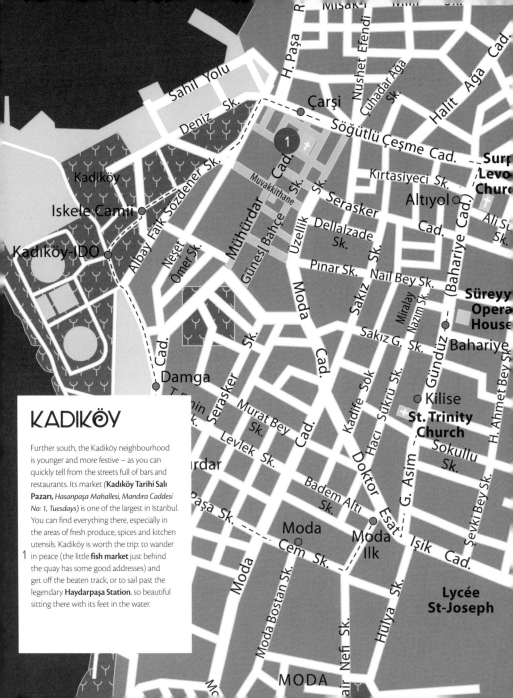

KADIKÖY

Further south, the Kadiköy neighbourhood is younger and more festive – as you can quickly tell from the streets full of bars and restaurants. Its market (**Kadıköy Tarihi Salı Pazarı,** *Hasanpaşa Mahallesi, Mandıra Caddesi No: 1, Tuesdays*) is one of the largest in Istanbul. You can find everything there, especially in the areas of fresh produce, spices and kitchen utensils. Kadıköy is worth the trip: to wander in peace (the little **fish market** just behind the quay has some good addresses) and get off the beaten track, or to sail past the legendary **Haydarpaşa Station**, so beautiful sitting there with its feet in the water.

LENTIL SOUP
mercimek çorbası

This dish is first among soups: the most common and popular in Turkey.

Preparation time: 10 minutes
Cooking time: 30 minutes
Serves 4
40 g (1½ oz) butter
1 onion, chopped
150 g (5½ oz/¾ cup) dried red lentils, picked over and rinsed
1 carrot, sliced into rounds
1 all-purpose potato (such as desiree), peeled and cut into chunks
1 tablespoon tomato paste (concentrated purée)
1 lemon, cut into wedges

Melt the butter in a large saucepan over medium heat. Add the onion and lentils, and cook, stirring, for 10 minutes, or until the onion is very soft. Next, add the carrot, potato, tomato paste and 1 litre (35 fl oz/4 cups) water. Season with salt and freshly ground black pepper. Cover and continue cooking for 20 minutes, or until the lentils and vegetables are very tender. Purée the soup in a blender or a food processor until smooth (add a little extra water if the soup is too thick). Return the soup to a clean pan to heat through once again. Serve hot with lemon wedges for squeezing over.

Note: You can add a little sauce to this dish by melting 30 g (1 oz) butter, adding 1 tablespoon dried mint and drizzling over the soup when serving.

CHICKEN SOUP
tavuk çorbası

If you have chicken left over from another meal, use it to make a soup. The first stock will be better if you add the chicken carcass and bones.

Preparation time: 5 minutes
Cooking time: 30 minutes
Serves 4
300 g (10½ oz) free-range skinless chicken breast fillets
50 g (1¾ oz) vermicelli noodles
50 g (1¾ oz) butter
50 g (1¾ oz/⅓ cup) plain (all-purpose) flour
1 small handful flat-leaf (Italian) parsley, chopped
1 small red chilli, seeded and finely chopped (optional)
1 lemon, cut into wedges

Simmer the chicken in 1 litre (35 fl oz/4 cups) salted water (even better with a few chicken bones or a carcass as well) in a large saucepan for about 20 minutes. Once cooked, remove the chicken meat from the poaching liquid, reserving the liquid (discard any bones/carcass if used), and chop the meat into small pieces. Return the chicken to the broth with the vermicelli, and turn off the heat. Melt the butter in a small saucepan over medium–low heat. Add the flour and cook, stirring with a wooden spoon, for 2 minutes, to cook out the flour taste. Gradually add a little of the chicken broth and the parsley. Add this sauce to the rest of the broth immediately. Heat through again, stirring, to thicken the soup. Serve hot, sprinkled with a little chilli (if using) and the lemon wedges for squeezing over.

TRIPE SOUP
işkembe çorbası

Tripe soup is a night-time soup, eaten very late or very early in the morning after being out all night. It is supposed to perk you up after a night of excess. In Istanbul, establishments specialising in tripe dishes (*işkembeci*) are open around the clock and are found in neighbourhoods that have a vibrant nightlife.

Preparation time: 10 minutes
Cooking time: 45 minutes
Serves 4

**400 g (14 oz) pre-cooked veal or sheep's tripe,
    cut into small squares (see note)**
40 g (1½ oz) butter
40 g (1½ oz) plain (all-purpose) flour
3 garlic cloves
60 ml (2 fl oz/¼ cup) red wine vinegar
pul biber (Aleppo pepper) or other chilli flakes (optional)

Bring 1 litre (35 fl oz/4 cups) salted water to the boil in a large saucepan. Add the tripe and simmer, covered, for 30 minutes. Skim off any foam that forms on the surface of the liquid. Melt the butter in a small saucepan over medium–low heat. Add the flour and a little salt, and cook, stirring with a wooden spoon, for 2 minutes, to cook out the taste of the flour. Gradually blend in some of the tripe broth (about 300 ml/10 fl oz), stirring with a whisk or wooden spoon. Once the sauce has thickened, pour it into the soup and continue to cook, stirring, for at least another 10 minutes. Crush the garlic using a mortar and pestle, and add it to the vinegar. Sprinkle the hot soup with the garlicky vinegar and chilli flakes to taste (if using) before serving.

Note: Pre-cooked tripe is available from good butchers or offal specialists, and practical for avoiding a lengthy cooking time.

TOMATO SOUP
domates çorbası

This simple soup is served in two ways: cold and dressed with olive oil in summer, and hot with butter in winter.

Preparation time: 20 minutes
Cooking time: 20 minutes
Serves 4
1 kg (2 lb 4 oz) tomatoes, blanched, peeled and quartered
1 teaspoon caster (superfine) sugar
extra virgin olive oil (cold version) or 40 g (1½ oz) butter (hot version)

Put the tomatoes in a large saucepan, and cover with lightly salted water. Add the sugar, and stir to dissolve. Cover the pan, and cook over medium heat for about 20 minutes until the tomatoes are soft. Purée the soup in a blender or food processor. Dress with a drizzle of olive oil if serving chilled or the melted butter if serving hot.

YOGHURT SOUP
yoğurt çorbası

When the universal rice meets the universal yoghurt, you end up with a filling soup that can serve as dinner all by itself.

Preparation time: 20 minutes
Cooking time: 20 minutes
Serves 4
200 g (7 oz/scant 1 cup) short-grain rice
500 g (1 lb 2 oz) Turkish or Greek-style yoghurt
40 g (1½ oz) butter
2 tablespoons dried mint
pul biber (Aleppo pepper) or other chilli flakes

In a large saucepan, simmer the rice in 1 litre (35 fl oz/4 cups) salted water for about 20 minutes (do not drain). Whisk the yoghurt in a bowl, and blend it gradually into the rice, mixing carefully, to make a smooth soup. Melt the butter, add the mint and pour the mixture over the soup. Sprinkle over the chilli flakes to season, and serve hot.

MEATBALLS
köfte

Meat for köfte must be well trimmed of any sinew and passed through the mincer twice. Choose fattier parts of the animal (boneless chuck for beef, neck for mutton) for flavour, and to help to hold the köfte together.

Preparation time: 20 minutes
Cooking time: 10 minutes
Serves 4 (about 16 meatballs)

1 slice day-old bread (about 50 g/1¾ oz)
500 g (1 lb 2 oz) beef (such as boneless
chuck), finely minced (ground)
by your butcher
1 small onion, finely chopped
1 small handful flat-leaf (Italian) parsley,
finely chopped
1 teaspoon ground cumin
olive oil for pan-frying, plus extra for greasing

Soak the bread in some water until it is thoroughly wet. Transfer to a sieve, and squeeze out any excess moisture by gently pushing down with your hands. Put the soaked bread in a large bowl, and add the beef, onion, parsley and cumin. Season with salt and freshly ground black pepper. Knead all the ingredients together for a while with your hands. Grease your hands with oil, and shape the mixture into balls the size of an egg (about 50 g/1¾ oz each) in the hollow of your palm, then flatten slightly. Heat a little olive oil in a large frying pan over medium heat, and cook the köfte for about 5 minutes on each side.

Variation: The meatballs (round, for a change) can be cooked in 250 ml (9 fl oz/1 cup) tomato passata (tomato purée), with peas and diced carrots sautéed first in olive oil.

STEAK TARTARE
çig köfte

Here, the most important thing is to choose meat that is very fresh – tell your butcher that you will be using it to make tartare, so that you will get the very best quality possible. While this recipe does not involve any cooking with heat, it does need to be mixed and kneaded for some time.

Preparation time: 40 minutes
Serves 4

250 g (9 oz) beef tenderloin, finely minced (ground) by your butcher
250 g (9 oz) fine burghul (bulgur)
1 large, well-ripened tomato, grated
2 bulb spring onions (scallions), grated
1 generous tablespoon tatlı biber salçası (mild Turkish chilli paste) (see page 34)
1 tablespoon tomato paste (concentrated purée)
1 teaspoon freshly ground black pepper
1 teaspoon ground allspice
½ teaspoon pul biber (Aleppo pepper) or other chilli flakes
a few mint and flat-leaf (Italian) parsley sprigs, leaves finely chopped

Put all the ingredients except the mint and parsley in a large bowl, season well with salt and knead together with your hands for a good 30 minutes. Add the parsley and mint, and knead for a further 2 minutes. Take a small handful of meat, and squeeze the mixture in your fist, leaving the mark of your fingers on the meatball you have made. Repeat until you have used all the mixture. Serve with crisp green lettuce leaves.

'LADY'S THIGHS'
kadın budu köfte

The name of this köfte translates as 'lady's thighs', and comes from its traditional shape; draw on your sculptural skills to make whatever shape you like along these lines.

Preparation time: 30 minutes
Cooking time: 30–40 minutes
Serves 4
50 g (1¾ oz/¼ cup) medium-grain rice
400 g (14 oz) minced (ground) chuck steak
1 egg
1 small onion, finely chopped
1 teaspoon ground allspice
1 teaspoon ground cinnamon
1 small handful dill, chopped
butter for pan-frying

Cook the rice in lightly salted water according to the packet instructions. Drain in a colander or sieve, and rinse under cold running water to cool it down; drain again. In a medium bowl, combine the cooled rice with the meat, egg, onion, spices and dill. Season with salt. Using both hands, knead all the ingredients together for a few minutes. Slap the ball of meat on a clean work surface five or six times to drive any air out of the mixture and make the meat very compact. Using your hands once again, shape into long meatballs (like a lady's thigh, obviously); you will end up with about 20 köfte. Melt a generous knob of butter in a large frying pan over medium heat. Pan-fry for about 10 minutes until the köfte are golden brown on both sides, working in batches so that you do not crowd the pan and adding more butter as needed. Serve hot.

BEEF DUMPLINGS
manti

Mantı: the unmissable little Armenian dumplings. They have their own special restaurants, *mantıcı*, and you can understand why. They are in a class of their own – a must-try and a must-make on a regular basis. Another way of preparing these is to cook them in water instead of the oven (if you want to try this, make them into small closed square packets).

Preparation time: 50 minutes
Resting time: 30 minutes
Cooking time: 20 minutes
Serves 4

DUMPLINGS
**250 g (9 oz/1⅔ cups) plain
(all-purpose) flour**
2 tablespoons sunflower oil
**400 g (14 oz) minced (ground)
beef (such as chuck)**
1 onion, grated

BROTH
**500 ml (17 fl oz/2 cups)
chicken or beef stock**
**1 tablespoon tomato paste
(concentrated purée)**

YOGHURT SAUCE
3 garlic cloves
**600 g (1 lb 5 oz) Turkish or
Greek-style yoghurt,
at room temperature
(remove from the
refrigerator 1 hour
before needed)**
2 tablespoons dried mint

Make the dumpling dough. Combine the flour, sunflower oil and a little water (about 150 ml/5 fl oz) to make a smooth dough. Wrap in a damp tea towel (dish towel) and leave to rest for 30 minutes at room temperature. Preheat the oven to 200°C (400°F). Mix together the stock and tomato paste for the broth. To make the filling for the dumplings, combine the meat and onion, making sure to mix evenly, and season with salt and freshly ground black pepper. Roll out the dumpling dough (as for a thin tart pastry), and cut into 6 cm (2½ inch) squares. Place a teaspoon of the meat filling in the middle of each square, and fold the filled dough into a boat shape (open in the middle, pinched together with your fingers at the ends). Arrange the dumplings, open side up, in an ovenproof dish. Pour in a few spoonfuls of the broth, and bake in the oven for 20 minutes. Halfway through the cooking time, pour a ladleful of broth into the dish. Meanwhile, make the yoghurt sauce. Crush the garlic with a little salt using a mortar and pestle. Add it to a tablespoon of the yoghurt in a bowl, before adding the rest of the yoghurt, so that the garlic mixes through evenly. Sprinkle over the dried mint, stir through and spoon the sauce over the dumplings when they come out of the oven. Serve hot.

SPICY MUTTON KEBABS
Adana kebab

'Kebab' simply means grilled food. Not so simply, the grilled food family in Turkey is enormous and not to be trifled with. *Ocakbaşı* are restaurants organised around a central grill, where kebabs are made in front of your eyes. 'The important thing is the meat!' explains Hamit, from **Zübeyir Ocakbaşı**, a benchmark institution in Istanbul. It has to be very good quality, obviously, and a little fatty: allow 30% sheep tail fat in the total weight cooked. Kebabs are served with a host of accompaniments: sliced cucumber and tomatoes, thinly sliced onions sprinkled with sumac, pul biber (Aleppo pepper), mint leaves, finely chopped tomato salad covered with chopped parsley, olive oil and lemon, cacık (yoghurt with cucumber), grilled tomatoes and capsicums (peppers), and a few pide (Turkish flatbreads), so that you can make your own little sandwiches.

'Adana' (named after the town it comes from) is the spicy version of kebab. To soften the heat of the chilli, you can serve it with ayran (drinking yoghurt, see page 204).

Preparation time: 10 minutes
Cooking time: 10–15 minutes
Serves 4 (8 skewers)
500 g (1 lb 2 oz) minced (ground) mutton (including 30% sheep tail fat) or 350 g (12 oz) minced mutton (with a little fat) plus 150 g (5½ oz) minced beef chuck
3 long red or green chillies, seeded and finely chopped
pul biber (Aleppo pepper) or other chilli flakes
8 skewers (if you use wooden skewers, remember to soak them in cold water for 30 minutes beforehand)

Put the meat, chillies and a pinch of chilli flakes in a bowl. Season with salt, and combine the mixture evenly. Mould onto each skewer in a long, flattish sausage shape (grease your hands lightly with a little sunflower oil, so the meat does not stick to them). Grill on a medium–hot barbecue or under a preheated grill (broiler) for 10–15 minutes, turning the kebabs over halfway through the cooking time, until cooked through. Serve hot with salad.

Variation: In Zübeyir Ocakbaşı, they always mix a little beef with the mutton. The house version of the spiced kebab (the beyti kebab) adds a large handful of flat-leaf (Italian) parsley, half a tomato and a garlic clove, all chopped very finely, to the Adana recipe. For a milder and simpler version (Urfa kebab), mix together minced (ground) mutton and beef, and season with salt – and a little freshly ground black pepper if you like.

Note: Sheep tail fat comes from the tail and hind fat of some breeds of sheep, and especially the fat-tailed sheep. It is used in Turkish and other Middle Eastern cuisines. Available as unrendered and rendered fat, it can be found at Middle Eastern or specialty butchers. Its use in this recipe is important because it helps to keep the kebabs moist and flavourful. If you cannot find it or it does not appeal, make sure to use a mince with a good percentage of fat in its content; lean mince is not suitable. You can ask your butcher to make the mince for you fresh.

VEAL WITH TOMATO

tas kebabı

Originally this dish was made with beef in a 'tas' (bowl). Here, we replace the more traditional beef with tender veal, and the bowl with a flameproof casserole (unless, of course, you have a flameproof bowl that can go on the stove).

Preparation time: 25 minutes
Cooking time: 55 minutes
Serves 4

30 g (1 oz) butter
1 onion, finely chopped
400 g (14 oz) veal, cut into cubes
1 tablespoon tomato paste
(concentrated purée)
2 tomatoes, blanched, peeled and diced
2 garlic cloves, crushed
1 tablespoon sweet paprika
2 large all-purpose potatoes
(such as desiree)
olive or peanut (groundnut) oil,
for deep-frying

Melt the butter in a medium flameproof casserole over medium heat. Add the onion and sauté for 5 minutes, or until soft and translucent. Next, add the meat and tomato paste, and continue to cook, stirring, for 5 minutes. Add the tomatoes, garlic, paprika and 250 ml (9 fl oz/1 cup) water. Season with salt and freshly ground black pepper. Cover and simmer gently for 45 minutes. Meanwhile, peel and cut the potatoes into chips (thick fries). Heat enough oil for deep-frying in a heavy-based frying pan over medium–high heat until it reaches 180°C (350°F), or a cube of bread dropped into the oil turns golden brown in 15 seconds. Carefully add the chips, in batches if necessary, and deep-fry for about 20 minutes, or until golden and crisp on the outside. Remove carefully with a slotted spoon to a plate lined with paper towel; add to the cooked meat just before serving. Mix together quickly without breaking up the chips. Serve hot.

EGGPLANT KEBABS
patlıcan kebabı

For this recipe try to find long eggplants, which are easy to cut into chunks and thread onto skewers with the meat. Otherwise, small eggplants will do the job. The important thing is to give them time to grill on the barbecue, so that their melting texture and smoky flavour combines with the flavour of the meat.

Preparation time: 15 minutes
Cooking time: 10–15 minutes
Serves 4

2–4 eggplants (aubergines)
500 g (1 lb 2 oz) minced (ground) mutton (including 30% sheep tail fat, see note page 100) or 350 g (12 oz) minced mutton (still with some fat) plus 150 g (5½ oz) minced beef chuck
8 skewers (if you use wooden skewers, remember to soak them in cold water for 30 minutes beforehand)

Discard the eggplant stalks, and cut each eggplant into six or eight chunky pieces. Season the meat with salt. Thread alternate pieces of eggplant and moulded portions of meat onto the skewers. Grill the skewers on a medium–hot barbecue or under a preheated grill (broiler) for 10–15 minutes, turning over halfway through the cooking time. Serve hot, wrapped in a pide or similar flatbread, with your choice of traditional accompaniments (see page 100).

SAUTÉED LAMB WITH SMOKY EGGPLANT
hünkar begendi

'The sovereign loved it.' This is the translation of 'hünkar begendi', referring to its origin – at least according to the story that attests the dish was invented in the seventeenth century for Sultan Murad IV. Two hundred years later, the Empress Eugénie, wife of Napoléon III, was also supposed to have especially enjoyed this dish. So, sovereigns do love it, then. And not only sovereigns – me, too. It can be made with either cubes of meat or as meatballs.

Preparation time: 50 minutes
Cooking time: 40 minutes
Serves 4

2 tablespoons sunflower oil
1 onion, very finely chopped
400 g (14 oz) boned lamb (such as boned short loin saddle),
    cut into cubes
40 g (1½ oz) butter
1 teaspoon sweet paprika
6 eggplants (aubergines) (choose ones that are not too large)
2 tablespoons olive oil
2 tablespoons plain (all-purpose) flour
200 ml (7 fl oz) milk
60 g (2¼ oz) kaşar, cantal or emmental cheese, grated
1 small handful flat-leaf (Italian) parsley, chopped

Heat the sunflower oil in a large frying pan over medium–high heat. Add the onion and sauté for about 5 minutes until soft. Now add the meat, season with freshly ground black pepper and brown for a few minutes over high heat. Cover, reduce the heat to low and continue cooking for about 30 minutes until the lamb is tender. Just before serving, season with salt. Melt the butter with the paprika in a small frying pan over medium heat; set aside to keep warm. Meanwhile, make the purée. Prick the eggplants and cook directly over a gas flame or under a preheated hot grill (broiler), turning regularly, until the flesh is meltingly soft. Open up each eggplant (use tongs if they are too hot to handle) and scrape out the flesh with a spoon (discard the skin). Mash the flesh to a purée with a fork; set aside. Stir the olive oil and flour in a medium saucepan over medium heat until the mixture turns a caramel colour. Gradually add the milk, then the eggplant purée and cheese, stirring continuously. Season with salt and pepper. Serve the purée hot, topped with the meat, drizzled with the paprika butter and with the parsley scattered over the top.

Note: Kaşar (known as kasseri in Greece) is an unpasteurised medium–hard cheese made from sheep's milk with a small amount of goat's milk mixed in. You can find it at Turkish, other Middle Eastern or Mediterranean food shops.

LAMB KEBABS
şiş kebab

'Şiş' is the skewer. At **Zübeyir Ocakbaşı**, they insist that the marinade not be too strong, so that it does not overpower the flavour of the meat.

Preparation time: 5 minutes
Marinating time: overnight
Cooking time: 10–15 minutes
Serves 4

600 g (1 lb 5 oz) lamb (such as boned shoulder and including 30% sheep tail fat, see note on page 100)
sunflower oil
pul biber (Aleppo pepper) or other chilli flakes
1 garlic clove, halved
12 skewers (if you use wooden skewers, remember to soak them in cold water for 30 minutes beforehand)

Massage the lamb with a generous amount of sunflower oil, seasoned with salt and chilli flakes. Cut the meat into rectangles about 2 x 4 cm (¾ x 1½ inches). Put the lamb pieces in a glass or ceramic dish, and cover with plastic wrap. Leave to marinate in the refrigerator overnight. The next day, before threading the pieces of lamb onto the skewers, rub them with the garlic. Assemble the kebabs, and grill on a medium–hot barbecue or under a preheated grill (broiler) for 10–15 minutes, turning them regularly so that they cook evenly. Serve hot.

VEAL KEBABS
simit kebab

A winter dish and a recipe from Hande Bozdoğan (see pages 164–165), who serves it with a burghul pilav (page 124) and a parsley salad (page 44). Simit kebab is a very popular dish in the Southeastern Anatolia region (Gaziantep province). 'Simit' is a local term for very fine burghul.

Preparation time: 20 minutes
Soaking time (burghul): 15 minutes
Cooking time: 10–15 minutes
Serves 4 (8 kebabs)
100 g (3½ oz) fine burghul (bulgur)
150 ml (5 fl oz) boiling water
1 teaspoon ground allspice
1 teaspoon ground cumin
1 teaspoon pul biber (Aleppo pepper) or other chilli flakes
1 teaspoon dried mint
100 g (3½ oz/¾ cup) crushed pistachio nut kernels
1 onion
2 garlic cloves
400 g (14 oz) minced (ground) veal escalopes or other
good-quality minced veal
sunflower oil
8 skewers (if you use wooden skewers, remember to soak
them in cold water for 30 minutes beforehand)

Put the burghul in a bowl. Cover with the boiling water, and leave to soak for 15 minutes, to allow the grains to swell. Drain off any excess water. Meanwhile, mix together the allspice, cumin, chilli flakes, dried mint and half the crushed nuts. Season with salt and freshly ground black pepper. Mix all of this with the soaked burghul. Grate the onion and garlic to extract their juices (discard any onion flesh that is left on the grater), and combine with the meat in a large bowl. Add this mixture to the spiced burghul mixture and mix well. Grease your hands with sunflower oil, and mould a handful of the mixture into a sausage shape around each skewer, to make eight kebabs. Grill for 10–15 minutes on a medium hot barbecue or under a preheated grill (broiler), turning, until cooked through. Sprinkle the kebabs with the rest of the crushed pistachios, and serve hot.

CHICKEN WINGS
kanat

You can find special ready-made spice mixes for chicken in Turkish or other Middle Eastern food shops. Otherwise, use ground allspice or quatre épices spice mix instead (see note below).

Preparation time: 15 minutes
Resting time: overnight
Cooking time: 15 or 30 minutes
Serves 4
1 garlic clove
1 onion, grated
2 tablespoons ready-made spice mix for poultry
pul biber (Aleppo pepper) or other chilli flakes
60 ml (2 fl oz/¼ cup) olive oil
250 g (9 oz) Turkish or Greek-style yoghurt
1 kg (2 lb 4 oz) free-range chicken wings

Crush the garlic with some salt using a mortar and pestle. In a small bowl, gently mix together the garlic, onion, spice mix, a good pinch of chilli flakes (or to taste), olive oil and yoghurt. Put the chicken wings in a glass or ceramic dish, and pour over the yoghurt marinade. Cover with plastic wrap, and leave to marinate in the refrigerator overnight. The next day, preheat the barbecue to medium–hot. Grill the chicken wings for about 15 minutes, turning so that they brown evenly, until cooked through. Alternatively, cook in a preheated oven at 200°C (400°F) for 30 minutes. Serve hot.

Note: Quatre épices, which translates from the French simply as 'four spices', is a spice mix found not only in French cooking, but also in the store cupboard of some Middle Eastern cuisines. It usually contains ground pepper (white, black, or both), cloves, nutmeg and ginger, and can be found in good delicatessens and some Middle Eastern food shops, as well as online from gourmet and other specialist food suppliers.

SAUTÉED LAMB'S LIVER
arnavut ciğeri

Tripe is not the only type of offal much beloved in Turkish cuisine. The number of offal specialists in Istanbul is large and the dishes varied. Lamb liver is one such classic. Always cook it at the last minute, to preserve the melt-in-your-mouth texture of the liver.

Preparation time: 10 minutes
Cooking time: 10 minutes
Serves 4
400 g (14 oz) lamb's liver, trimmed and any veins removed
vinegar (such as apple cider or red wine vinegar)
1 teaspoon sweet paprika
pul biber (Aleppo pepper) or other chilli flakes (see page 36)
50 g (1¾ oz) butter
1 lemon, cut into wedges, or pomegranate molasses
    (available from Turkish or other Middle Eastern food
    shops, some supermarkets or online), to serve

Clean the liver with some vinegar. Rinse in a colander under cold running water, then pat dry with paper towel. Cut into large cubes, and put in a bowl. Season with salt, add the paprika and a large pinch of chilli flakes, and mix together by hand. Melt the butter in a large frying pan over high heat. Once sizzling, add the liver and sauté for 2–3 minutes, being careful not to overcook (otherwise the liver will be tough). Serve immediately with rice and some lemon wedges for squeezing over, or dressed with a little pomegranate molasses.

LAMB STEW
kuzu güveç

Güveç has a lot going for it: You use whichever vegetables you like, all the ingredients go into the one pot, you bake it for a while and, voilà, it is ready. Tasty, easy and practical.

Preparation time: 20 minutes
Soaking time (eggplants): 30 minutes
Cooking time: 4 hours
Serves 6

2 small eggplants (aubergines)
800 g (1 lb 12 oz) lamb shoulder, cut into cubes (you can ask your
**   butcher to do this, and make sure to reserve the bones for cooking)**
1 zucchini (courgette), diced
2 carrots, sliced into rounds
2 all-purpose potatoes (such as desiree), peeled and diced
1 small red capsicum (pepper), seeded and diced
1 small green capsicum (pepper), seeded and diced
2 onions, sliced into rounds
2 tomatoes, halved

Remove the stems from the eggplants, cut the eggplants into cubes and put them in a bowl. Cover with salted water and leave to soak for 30 minutes, then squeeze out and pat dry with paper towel or a clean tea towel (dish towel). Preheat the oven to 180°C (350°F). In a large earthenware ovenproof dish (or a large flameproof casserole), arrange layers of ingredients: first the meat (and at least one bone), then the zucchini, carrots, eggplants, potatoes, capsicums, onions and tomatoes. Pour over 200 ml (7 fl oz) water, and season with salt and a little freshly ground black pepper. Cover and cook in the oven for 4 hours, or until the meat is meltingly tender and all the flavours have melded.

SPINACH WITH RICE
ispanak pirinçleme

If you like, the spinach here can be swapped out for
diced zucchini (courgette).

Preparation time: 20 minutes
Cooking time: 20 minutes
Serves 4
200 g (7 oz/scant 1 cup) medium-grain rice
60 ml (2 fl oz/¼ cup) olive oil
2 onions, finely chopped
300 g (10½ oz) good-quality minced (ground) beef (ask your
butcher to do this so that it is as fresh as possible)
600 g (1 lb 5 oz) English spinach, washed and chopped

Rinse the rice in several changes of cold water. Heat the olive oil in a
large frying pan or large flameproof casserole over medium heat. Quickly
sauté the onions, meat and rice for a few minutes until the onion has
softened and the rice grains are coated in the oil. Add the spinach
and cook, stirring, for 3 minutes, then pour in 750 ml (26 fl oz/3 cups)
water. Season with salt, cover and continue cooking for 15–20 minutes,
keeping at a simmer, until the rice has absorbed nearly all the water.
Remove from the heat and leave to rest, covered and undisturbed, for
a further 5–10 minutes, so that the rice absorbs the rest of the liquid.

RICE PILAV AND RICE WITH VERMICELLI

pilav and şehriyeli pilav

You can make a plain pilav and easily liven it up with chopped onions, pine nuts, raisins, cooked chickpeas or your choice of vegetables, sautéed in the butter with the rice before adding the water.

The principle of making a good pilav is to sauté the rice in some butter (or oil), before cooking it, covered, with just the amount of water it needs (without draining) – which is to say, one-and-a-half to two times the volume of rice. A little trick for making it even better is to let the rice rest once cooked, still covered, for about 10 minutes (off the heat) so it continues to swell. Pilav is traditionally made using white rice, though you can adapt it to your choice of rice. Remember that you may have to allow for faster or slower absorption rates, or more or less starch (it is worth rinsing high-starch rices thoroughly).

Here is a very simple pilav. Remember, if you should need to add water during the cooking time, make sure that it is boiling, so it does not interrupt the cooking process.

Preparation time: 5 minutes
Resting time (rice): 30 minutes
Cooking time: 20 minutes
Serves 4
360 g (12¾ oz/1⅔ cups) medium-grain rice
40 g (1½ oz) butter
40 g (1½ oz) vermicelli noodles (a big handful)

Put the rice in a medium bowl, cover with hot water and leave to soak for 30 minutes. Drain in a colander, then rinse several times; set aside. Melt the butter in a large, lidded frying pan or medium flameproof casserole over medium heat. Add the vermicelli and sauté for a few minutes until golden. Next, add the rice, season with salt and continue to cook, stirring, for a few minutes until the rice grains are well coated in the butter. Pour in 750 ml (26 fl oz/3 cups) water (or 1 litre/35 fl oz/4 cups, depending on the rice used; 750 ml will be enough in most cases). Cover and continue cooking for about 15 minutes until the rice has absorbed nearly all the water. Remove the pan or casserole from the heat, keep covered and leave the rice to finish swelling, undisturbed, for a further 10 minutes.

THIS PILAV IS AN INSTITUTION, ONE THAT IS OFTEN SERVED ALONGSIDE MAIN DISHES. THE TERM 'PILAV' DOES NOT REFER TO THE RICE AS SUCH, BUT TO THE WAY OF COOKING IT.

TOMATO PILAV
domatesli pilav

Here's another way of making pilav. Soaking the rice in water for half a day before cooking means that the water needed to cook the rice is almost half the amount used in the traditional version (the equivalent of the volume of rice), as the rice has already had its fill of water. This results in a wonderfully tender grain.

Preparation time: 5 minutes
Resting time (rice): at least 6 hours
Cooking time: 10 minutes
Serves 4
360 g (12¾ oz/1⅗ cups) medium-grain rice
40 g (1½ oz) butter
4 large tomatoes, grated (discard any skin that remains on the grater)

Half a day before cooking, put the rice in a large bowl and cover well with water. Leave the rice to soak until needed, then drain in a colander and rinse the rice several times to remove the starch; set aside to drain. Bring 500 ml (17 fl oz/2 cups) water to the boil. Melt the butter in a separate large saucepan, add the tomatoes and drained rice, and season with salt. Cook, stirring, for 2 minutes. Add the boiling water, cover and continue cooking over medium heat for 10 minutes. After this time, the water will have been almost completely absorbed by the rice – although it will still be quite moist. Remove the saucepan from the heat, keep covered and leave the rice to finish swelling, undisturbed, for a further 10 minutes.

BURGHUL PILAV
bulgur pilavı

When dressed with a little olive oil instead of butter, this burghul pilav also works as a cold salad in summer.

Preparation time: 10 minutes
Cooking time: 20 minutes
Serves 4
60 ml (2 fl oz/¼ cup) olive oil
2 onions, finely diced
1 garlic clove, finely chopped
pul biber (Aleppo pepper) or other chilli flakes
1 tablespoon tomato paste (concentrated purée)
200 g (7 oz) coarse burghul (bulgur)
500 ml (17 fl oz/2 cups) boiling water
20 g (¾ oz) butter

Heat the olive oil in a large frying pan over medium–high heat. Add the onions, garlic and chilli flakes to taste, and season with salt. Sauté for 5 minutes, or until the onion is soft. Add the tomato paste and burghul, and continue to cook, stirring, for a further 5 minutes. Pour the boiling water over the burghul in the pan. Reduce the heat to medium, cover and continue cooking for 10 minutes. Dot the butter on top of the hot pilav just before serving.

CHICKEN PILAV
içli pilav

The 'içli' in this dish's name refers to the inside –
traditionally the chicken is stuffed with the rice.

Preparation time: 20 minutes
Cooking time: about 2 hours
Serves 4
30 g (1 oz) butter
1 free-range whole chicken, about 1.5 kg (3 lb 5 oz)
2 tablespoons sunflower oil
2 onions, finely diced
360 g (12¾ oz/1⅔ cups) medium-grain rice
1 generous tablespoon ground cinnamon
1 generous tablespoon ground allspice
100 g (3½ oz/⅔ cup) pine nuts
100 g (3½ oz/⅔ cup) currants
1 large handful dill, finely chopped

Melt the butter in a large flameproof casserole (large enough to hold
the chicken easily) over medium heat. Add the chicken, and brown on
all sides for about 10 minutes until the skin has taken on a good colour.
Pour in 200 ml (7 fl oz) water, cover the casserole and cook the chicken
for about 1½ hours (more or less, depending on its size). Set the chicken
aside to keep warm, and reserve the liquid for cooking the rice. Heat
the sunflower oil in a large frying pan over medium–high heat. Add the
onions and sauté for 5 minutes, or until soft. Add the rice, cinnamon,
allspice, pine nuts and currants, and season with salt. Cook, stirring, for a
further 5 minutes over medium heat. Add enough water to the reserved
chicken broth to make 750 ml (26 fl oz/3 cups). Pour over the rice, cover
and continue cooking for about 15 minutes until the rice has absorbed
nearly all the liquid. Remove the saucepan from the heat, keep covered
and leave the rice to finish swelling, undisturbed, for a further 10 minutes.
Sprinkle the dill over the pilav just before serving with the warm chicken.

SEA BASS PILAV
levrekli pilav

This dish, sampled at **Delicatessen** (see pages 130–131),
brings together several essential elements of Istanbulite
gastronomy including fish, nuts and rice. Here, the
crunchy almonds, pine nuts and pistachios end up
being as soft as the pilav in which they are cooked.

Preparation time: 20 minutes
Resting time (rice): 30 minutes
Cooking time: 45 minutes
Serves 4
250 g (9 oz) sea bass or barramundi fillets (skin removed)
3 tablespoons olive oil
200 g (7 oz/scant 1 cup) medium-grain rice
150 g (5½ oz) mixed almonds, pistachio nut kernels and pine nuts
20 g (¾ oz) butter
1 large handful flat-leaf (Italian) parsley, leaves finely chopped,
    plus extra, cut into fine strips, for serving
20 mint leaves, finely chopped

Coat the fish fillets with 2 tablespoons of the olive oil, season with salt and
set aside. Put the rice in a small bowl, cover with hot water and leave to
soak for 30 minutes; drain in a colander or sieve, and rinse several times
with fresh cold water. Meanwhile, preheat the oven to 180°C (350°F).
Arrange the nuts in a single layer on a baking tray, and toast in the oven for
about 8 minutes until golden. Set aside; do not turn off the oven. Melt the
butter with the remaining 1 tablespoon of oil in a frying pan over medium
heat. Add the rice and sauté for 5 minutes, or until all the grains are well
coated in the butter-oil mixture. Add 400 ml (14 fl oz) lightly salted water,
and cook over low heat for about 15 minutes until the rice has absorbed
the water. Add the toasted nuts, parsley and mint, and continue cooking,
stirring from time to time, for a further 2 minutes. Remove from the heat.
Arrange three-quarters of the fish fillets in a layer on the bottom of a
large, round ovenproof dish. Cover with the pilav, and finish by topping
with the rest of the fish. Sprinkle with a tablespoon of water, and bake
in the oven for 15 minutes. Serve hot, scattered with the extra parsley.

ELIF YALIN

Chef, *Mangerie* (Bebek)
and *Delicatessen* (Nişantaşı)

Ten years ago Elif Yalın opened her first restaurant in Istanbul: *Mangerie*, in the chic neighbourhood of Bebek. Then came another, *Delicatessen*, in the bustling neighbourhood of Nişantaşı. Both of these establishments are elegant, open to the street and lively, just like their chef, who reinterprets Turkish food to offer a delicate new cuisine that is all her own. In her dishes, she says, you find the Black Sea where she comes from, the seasons and her instinct. She is inspired by tradition, and by the present as well.

ELIF'S RECIPES
levrekli pilav (sea bass pilav, page 128), *Delicatessen* yufka böreği (little börek, page 170)

ADDRESSES
Mangerie, Cevdet Paşa Caddesi No: 69, Bebek
Delicatessen, Mim Kemal Öke Caddesi No: 19/1, Nişantaşı

AT
HOME

FAMILY RECIPES

In Istanbul homes, people cook. They make the classics you find on menus at the city's restaurants, but above all they cook dishes rooted in their family's origins. What makes Istanbul special is that it brings together all of the country's regions, specialities and customs. Now Turkey's economic centre, Istanbul is home to more than 15 million inhabitants and attracts Turks from all corners of the country. Until Ankara took over the title in 1923, Istanbul was the political capital not just of Turkey, but the Ottoman Empire as well. Before that still, it was called Byzantium, then Constantinople, and it was the capital of the Eastern Roman Empire – an early international city. You can find everything in Istanbul. This is also the case when it comes to food: from Van to Urfa in the east, and Antakya to Adana in the south, via the Black Sea, the Aegean Sea or the Mediterranean, you quickly move between the dishes of the coast and the very different cooking traditions of the inland. There are the butter devotees and those who cook only with olive oil, the residents of the coastal regions spoiled for choice when it comes to fruit and vegetables, and the people of the Anatolian towns who have made grains and meats their speciality. There are many contrasts in Turkey, but everywhere, and at all times, it is a point of honour that home-made dishes be not only very good (of course!), but also beautiful to look at, thoughtfully arranged and colourful – a visual feast.

ZUCCHINI FRITTERS
mücver

A family dish that is a great classic of Turkish cooking and one capable of converting even the most hardened zucchini hater. This recipe is the one used at **Lokanta Maya** (see pages 178–179), asked for by so many customers that one day Didem Şenol finally wrote it on the mirror of her restaurant.

Preparation time: 15 minutes
Resting time (zucchini): 1 hour
Cooking time: 15 minutes
Serves 4
1 kg (2 lb 4 oz) zucchini (courgettes)
200 g (7 oz/1⅓ cups) plain (all-purpose) flour
4 eggs
2 large handfuls dill, finely chopped
2 large handfuls flat-leaf (Italian) parsley, finely chopped
8 bulb spring onions (scallions), finely chopped
150 g (5½ oz) beyaz peynir (Turkish white cheese,
**   see page 14) or feta cheese, crumbled**
400 ml (14 fl oz) olive or peanut (groundnut) oil for shallow-frying
YOGHURT SAUCE
3 tablespoons Turkish or Greek-style yoghurt
a few coriander (cilantro) leaves, finely chopped

Grate the zucchini into a sieve or colander set over a bowl, salt it and leave to disgorge any liquid for at least 1 hour (press down on the zucchini with a plate as needed, to extract the liquid). Put the flour in a large bowl and season with freshly ground black pepper. Add the eggs, and whisk together to combine. Put the zucchini in a separate bowl, and add the dill, parsley and spring onions. Next, add the cheese, stir through and combine evenly with the egg-flour mixture: you now have a fritter batter. Heat the oil for shallow-frying in a large heavy-based saucepan or deep frying pan over medium heat. Once the oil is hot, working in batches, carefully drop in tablespoons of the batter. Shallow-fry for a few minutes until crisp and golden all over. Remove carefully with a slotted spoon to a plate lined with paper towel; keep warm. Continue in this way until all the batter has been used, being careful not to crowd the pan. To make the sauce, whisk the yoghurt in a small bowl. Season with a little salt, and add the coriander leaves. Serve the fritters warm, with the yoghurt sauce for dipping.

ARTICHOKE HEARTS
IN OLIVE OIL
zeytinyağlı enginar

A fresh dish typical of the region of Turkey near the
Aegean Sea, where the many and varied vegetables
available are naturally cooked with olive oil.

Preparation time: 10 minutes
Cooking time: 30 minutes
Serves 4

8 artichoke hearts, trimmed and 'hairy' chokes removed
1 bulb spring onion (scallion), roughly chopped
   (keep white and green parts separate)
2 carrots, diced
1 all-purpose potato (such as desiree), diced
3 tablespoons olive oil
1 tablespoon plain (all-purpose) flour
1 teaspoon caster (superfine) sugar
juice of ½ lemon

Arrange the artichoke hearts in a large frying pan with the green parts of the
spring onion. Place a little of each of the carrots, potatoes and white parts of
the spring onion in the middle of each heart. Add 500 ml (17 fl oz/2 cups)
water, and season with salt. In a small bowl, lightly whisk together the olive
oil, flour and sugar. Pour over the artichoke hearts, cover and cook over
medium heat for about 30 minutes until the artichokes are tender. Transfer
to a large plate for serving, scattering the green spring onion from the pan
over the top. Serve lukewarm or cold.

BURGHUL BALLS
bulgurlu köfte

Köfte in the form of a vegetarian amuse-bouche. Very, very good!

Preparation time: 25 minutes
Cooking time: 20 minutes
Serves 4–6
4 all-purpose potatoes (such as bintje/yellow finn or desiree)
200 g (7 oz) fine burghul (bulgur) or semolina
3 tablespoons olive oil, plus extra for drizzling
2 bulb spring onions (scallions), chopped
1 handful flat-leaf (Italian) parsley, finely chopped
1 handful mint, finely chopped
pul biber (Aleppo pepper) or other chilli flakes
   (see note page 36)
juice of 1 lemon

Peel the potatoes, put in a medium saucepan and cover well with water. Add a little salt, bring to the boil and cook until tender to the point of a knife. Meanwhile, in a separate saucepan, bring 500 ml (17 fl oz/2 cups) salted water to the boil. Tip in the burghul, and reduce the heat to a simmer. Once the burghul has absorbed all the water, cover the pan, remove from the heat and set aside. Heat the 3 tablespoons olive oil in a large frying pan over medium heat. Add the spring onions and sauté for 3 minutes; remove from the heat. Next, add the parsley, mint and a generous pinch of chilli flakes or to taste. Season with salt. Drain the potatoes, and mash to a purée (use a little of the cooking water if needed). Once all the ingredients have cooled slightly (so you don't burn yourself), combine and knead together in a large bowl. Shape into small balls between your palms. Serve warm or cold, sprinkled with lemon juice and an extra drizzle of olive oil.

SAUTÉED EGGPLANT AND CAPSICUM
köpoğlu

To reduce the bitterness of the eggplant, soak it in salted water for 30 minutes.

Preparation time: 15 minutes
Soaking time (eggplants): 30 minutes
Cooking time: 20 minutes
Serves 4

2 eggplants (aubergines)
250 ml (9 fl oz/1 cup) sunflower oil
1 red capsicum (pepper), seeded and cut into squares
1 green capsicum (pepper), seeded and cut into squares
2 garlic cloves, grated
3 tomatoes, diced
125 g (4½ oz) Turkish or Greek-style yoghurt

Peel and dice the eggplants, and put in a large bowl. Cover with salted water, and leave to soak for 30 minutes; squeeze the pieces out well and pat dry with paper towel. Heat the sunflower oil in a large frying pan over medium–high heat. Add the eggplant, and sauté for 8–10 minutes until they soften and start to brown. Move to a plate, return the pan to the heat then add the capsicums (which brown much more quickly). Remove them in turn from the frying pan (put on some paper towel to drain off any excess oil). In the same pan, sauté the garlic for a minute or so, then add the tomatoes and cook over medium heat for 5 minutes, or until softened and starting to break down. Arrange the eggplant and capsicum in a dish, then top with the tomatoes. In a small bowl, whisk the yoghurt with a little salt. Once the vegetables have cooled, top with the yoghurt and serve.

FRIED VEGETABLE SALAD
şakşuka

Here it is, the Turkish answer to ratatouille and a dish that is cooked all along the Mediterranean coast. When preparing it, try to ensure the vegetables are all diced a similar size.

Preparation time: 5 minutes
Resting time: 30 minutes
Cooking time: 10 minutes
Serves 4

2 eggplants (aubergines), stalks removed
200 ml (7 fl oz) olive oil
2 small zucchini (courgettes), diced
2 long green capsicums (peppers), seeded and diced
1 garlic clove
500 ml (17 fl oz/2 cups) tomato passata (puréed tomatoes)

Halve the eggplants lengthways. Put cut side up in a sieve or colander set over a bowl, and sprinkle with salt. Leave for 30 minutes to disgorge any juices. Wipe the eggplants dry with paper towel, then dice them. Heat the olive oil in a large frying pan over medium–high heat. Add the eggplants, zucchini and capsicums, and sauté until lightly browned; work in batches if needed, so that the vegetables sauté, rather than stew. Remove from the pan and drain on paper towel. Meanwhile, crush the garlic with a little salt using a mortar and pestle. Put the garlic in a medium saucepan with the tomato passata, and cook, stirring, for 5 minutes over medium heat. Transfer the fried vegetables to a serving dish, and dress with the tomato sauce. Serve cold.

LENTIL BALLS
mercimek köfte

Here's another vegetarian version of köfte. There's an unforgettable version of this dish at **Namlı Gurme** (see page 27), in Karaköy, which overlooks the Aya Sofya and the skyline of Sultanahmet on the other side of the Galata Bridge. There are as many customers as there are dishes on the menu (and that's a lot!).

Preparation time: 20 minutes
Cooking time: 25 minutes
Serves 4–6

100 g (3½ oz/½ cup) split red lentils, picked over and rinsed
200 g (7 oz) fine burghul (bulgur)
10 g (¼ oz) butter
3 tablespoons olive oil
½ onion, finely chopped
2 garlic cloves
1 generous teaspoon tatlı biber salçası (mild
**   Turkish chilli paste, see page 34)**
pinch of pul biber (Aleppo pepper) or other chilli flakes
**   (see page 36)**
½ teaspoon ground cumin
½ teaspoon köfte spice mix (available from Turkish or
**   other Middle Eastern food shops) or ground allspice**
**   or quatre épices spice mix (see page 112)**
2 large handfuls flat-leaf (Italian) parsley, very finely chopped
3 or 4 bulb spring onions (scallions), very finely chopped
lettuce leaves, to serve
2 lemons, cut into wedges

Pour the lentils and 400 ml (14 fl oz) cold water into a medium–large saucepan. Cover and bring to the boil, then reduce the heat and continue cooking for 15–20 minutes until the lentils are very tender. Turn off the heat and add the burghul. Stir, cover and allow the burghul to swell in the residual heat of the lentils. Melt the butter with the olive oil in a small saucepan over medium heat. Add the onion and sauté for about 5 minutes until soft. Crush the garlic with a little salt using a mortar and pestle. Add to the onion in the pan with the chilli paste, chilli flakes and spices. Season with a little more salt if needed, and mix everything together over low heat for 2 minutes until fragrant. Next, add the parsley and spring onions to the lentil mixture. Stir everything together until smooth and evenly mixed. Take a plum-sized portion of the mixture in your hand, and shape into small quenelles, lightly imprinted with the mark of your fingers where they close on it. Serve warm with lettuce leaves and lemon wedges for squeezing over.

AICHA'S SALAD
Ayşe salatası

Making a Turkish meal can take a long time, several days even. Not just because some recipes take a little while to make, but rather because a multitude of meze is required for a crowd of guests. 'And in 5 minutes, it's all gone,' Ayşe ('Aicha') explains to me, laughing. This quick and easy salad is her creation. Thank you, Ayşe.

Preparation time: 10 minutes
Cooking time: 10 minutes
Serves 4
2 tablespoons sunflower oil
2 large zucchini (courgettes), grated
1 carrot, grated
2 garlic cloves
150 g (5½ oz) Turkish or Greek-style yoghurt
a few mint leaves, cut into fine strips
extra virgin olive oil, to serve

Heat the sunflower oil in a large frying pan over medium heat. Add the zucchini and carrot, and sauté for 10 minutes. Meanwhile, crush the garlic with a little salt using a mortar and pestle. Add it to a tablespoon of the yoghurt in a small bowl, before adding the rest of the yoghurt, so that the garlic mixes through evenly. Dress the vegetables with the yoghurt sauce, then add the mint leaves and a generous glug of olive oil.

HARICOT BEANS AND LAMB IN A TOMATO SAUCE
kuru fasulye

The cheap and versatile haricot bean makes a regular appearance
in Istanbul homes. Here, it is turned into a hearty winter stew ...

Preparation time: 30 minutes
Soaking time (beans): at least 12 hours
Cooking time: 55 minutes
Serves 4
200 g (7 oz/1 cup) dried haricot (navy) beans
40 g (1½ oz) butter
1 onion, chopped
2 tablespoons tomato paste (concentrated purée)
200 g (7 oz) lamb neck (with bones), chopped into
    pieces, or ready-cut lamb neck chops

The day before, soak the beans in a large volume of water. The next day,
drain and rinse with fresh cold water. Put the beans in a large saucepan,
cover well with water and bring to the boil. Simmer for about 20 minutes.
Drain again, cool a little, then remove and discard the loosened skins; set
the beans aside. Melt the butter in a large saucepan over medium heat.
Add the onion, tomato paste and lamb (with bones), and sauté for
5 minutes, or until the meat has browned and the onion is starting to
soften. Pour in 750 ml (26 fl oz/3 cups) water, and add the beans. Cover
and continue cooking at a low simmer for a good 30 minutes. Season with
salt and freshly ground black pepper just before serving. (Hot! with a pilav,
see page 120.)

HARIC❂T BEAN SALAD
piyaz

... And here, haricot beans make a fresh and filling
summer salad.

Preparation time: 15 minutes
Soaking time (beans): overnight
Cooking time: 1 hour
Serves 4
200 g (7 oz/1 cup) dried haricot (navy) beans
2 tomatoes, diced
1 onion, chopped
1 handful flat-leaf (Italian) parsley, chopped
juice of 1 lemon
3 tablespoons extra virgin olive oil

The day before, soak the beans in a large volume of water. The next
day, drain and rinse with fresh cold water. Put in a large saucepan,
cover well with water and bring to the boil. Simmer for a good hour
(or 30 minutes in a pressure cooker). Drain in a colander, cool a little,
then remove and discard the loosened skins; leave the beans to cool
completely. Combine the tomatoes, onion and parsley with the cold
beans. Dress with the lemon juice and olive oil, and season with salt.

BLACK-EYED PEAS WITH TOMATO

zeytinyağlı kuru börülce

Vegetable dishes cooked with olive oil (indicated by the 'zeytinyağlı' in the name) come from the south coast of Turkey. A little sugar is added and, while the dishes of these fertile regions are as varied as the vegetables they grow, they do share a gentle sweet–savoury note.

Preparation time: 10 minutes
Cooking time: 45 minutes
Serves 4
200 g (7 oz/1 cup) dried black-eyed peas
3 tablespoons olive oil
2 bulb spring onions (scallions), white part only, chopped
1 teaspoon caster (superfine) sugar
250 ml (9 fl oz/1 cup) tomato passata (puréed tomatoes)
1 tablespoon tomato paste (concentrated purée)

Put the black-eyed peas in a large saucepan, and cover well with water. Bring to the boil then turn down and simmer for 30 minutes, or until the beans are al dente; skim off any grey scum that forms on the surface as they cook. Drain in a colander. Meanwhile, heat the olive oil in a separate large saucepan over medium heat. Add the spring onions, sugar and a little salt, and sauté for 5 minutes, or until the onions are soft and tender. Pour in 300 ml (10½ fl oz) water, and stir through the tomato passata and tomato paste. Add the black-eyed peas to the mixture in the pan, and stir together. Cover and continue cooking at a gentle simmer for 15 minutes, taking care that the beans do not catch on the bottom of the pan. Serve hot.

BRAISED CELERY
zeytinyağlı kereviz

Vegetables are commonly served with meat and rice dishes in Turkish cuisine. You can also serve them as stand-alone dishes in the summer.

Preparation time: 15 minutes
Cooking time: 45 minutes
Serves 4
1 young whole celery (not too large)
2 all-purpose potatoes (such as desiree)
2 carrots, sliced into rounds
2 onions, thinly sliced
100 ml (3½ fl oz) olive oil
1 teaspoon caster (superfine) sugar
juice of ½ lemon

Slice the celery head into rounds and cut the stems (with their small leaves) into 2 cm (¾ inch) lengths. Peel and dice the potatoes. Put all the vegetables in a large frying pan, pour over a good drizzle of olive oil, and add the lemon juice and sugar. Season with salt, and add enough water to come just to the top of the vegetables. Cover and cook over medium–high heat for 45 minutes, or until the vegetables are quite tender.

BRAISED ZUCCHINI
kabak kavurma

When a little lightness is in order.

Preparation time: 5 minutes
Cooking time: 20 minutes
Serves 4

3 tablespoons olive oil
1 onion, finely chopped
4 zucchini (courgettes), diced
2 garlic cloves, finely chopped
1 teaspoon caster (superfine) sugar

Heat the olive oil in a large frying pan over medium heat. Add the onion and sauté for 5 minutes, or until soft. Next, add the zucchini, garlic and sugar, and season with salt. Keep cooking for 10–15 minutes until the zucchini is tender.

LEEKS IN OLIVE OIL
zeytinyağlı pırasa

Allspice is a very gentle, perfumed pepper-like spice, with a hint of clove. Together with cinnamon, it forms the most common duo of spices found in Turkish vegetable dishes, meats and pilavs. Do not hesitate to make this leek dish well ahead of serving time, as it is best enjoyed cold.

Preparation time: 10 minutes
Cooking time: 30 minutes
Resting time: at least 1 hour
Serves 4

1 kg (2 lb 4 oz) leeks, white parts only, sliced into rounds (reserve the green parts for another use – making stock perhaps)
100 g (3½ oz/½ cup) medium-grain rice
125 ml (4 fl oz/½ cup) olive oil
juice of ½ lemon
1 teaspoon ground cinnamon
1 teaspoon ground allspice
1 teaspoon caster (superfine) sugar

Put the leeks in a large saucepan, and add just enough water to reach the top of the vegetables, not cover them. Add the rice, olive oil, lemon juice, cinnamon, allspice and sugar. Season with salt. Cover and cook for about 30 minutes over medium heat. Leave to rest for at least 1 hour before serving cold.

STUFFED VINE LEAVES

sarma

'Sarma' refers to dishes made from leaves (vine, cabbage, silverbeet/Swiss chard ...) wrapped around a filling of spiced rice and herbs. The traditional recipe combines rice, onions, dried mint, lemon and olive oil. Hande Bozdoğan (see pages 164–165) gave me this sweet recipe. Sarma are best made the day before, and served cold.

SIMPLE SARMA

Preparation time: 1 hour 30 minutes
Cooking time: 1 hour 30 minutes
Resting time: at least 4 hours
Serves 6–8
60 ml (2 fl oz/¼ cup) olive oil, plus extra for baking
3 large onions, chopped
160 g (5¾ oz/1 cup) pine nuts
2 tablespoons caster (superfine) sugar
160 g (5¾ oz/1 cup) currants
240 g (8½ oz/generous 1 cup) medium-grain rice
160 g (5¾ oz/1 cup) sour cherries, pitted (optional)
3 teaspoons ground allspice
about 40 vine or small silverbeet (Swiss chard)
leaves, plus about 10 for the cooking process
2 lemons, 1 sliced and 1 cut into half-wedges

Heat the 60 ml (2 fl oz/¼ cup) olive oil in a large saucepan over medium heat. Add the onions and pine nuts, and sauté gently for 15 minutes, or until the onions are soft and the pine nuts golden. Add the sugar and currants, and sauté for a further 2 minutes. Tip in the rice, and cook over medium heat, stirring, for about 10 minutes. Mix in the sour cherries (if using) and allspice, and season with salt and freshly ground black pepper. Continue to cook, stirring, for another 5 minutes. Add 250 ml (9 fl oz/1 cup) water. Reduce the heat to low, cover and wait until the rice has absorbed all of the liquid (about 10 minutes). Remove from the heat and allow to cool, covered. Preheat the oven to 200°C

(400°F). Blanch the vine leaves in boiling water for 2 minutes, then refresh in cold water. Take about 40 leaves, and place a generous tablespoon of rice filling in the middle of each one, horizontally. Fold the right and left sides of the leaf over the filling, then take the bottom of the leaf and roll up fairly tightly towards the top. Use the lemon slices to cover the bottom of a large ovenproof dish (just big enough to fit the vine rolls snugly), add a few extra vine leaves, then the rolls on top, arranged in tight rows. Cover with more leaves, and pour 100 ml (3½ fl oz) water (or cherry juice from the jar or tin) and some extra olive oil on top. Cover with foil, and bake in the oven for 45 minutes. Allow to cool for at least 4 hours. Serve cold, with the lemon half-wedges for squeezing over.

Note: If you use vine leaves preserved in brine (easier to find than fresh ones), blanch in boiling water for 1 minute only; handle them with care, as they are fragile little things.

MEAT SARMA

Makes 25 sarma
200 g (7 oz) minced (ground) meat with a good proportion
of fat (such as chuck steak mixed with mutton)
55 g (2 oz/¼ cup) short-grain rice
1 generous tablespoon tomato paste (concentrated purée)
1 teaspoon tatlı biber salçası (mild Turkish
chilli paste, see page 34)
1 garlic clove, crushed
25 vine leaves, plus about 10 for the cooking process
olive oil

Combine all the ingredients except the vine leaves and olive oil in a large bowl. Season with salt and freshly ground black pepper. Use to stuff the vine leaves, blanched beforehand (as explained in the recipe above). Line the bottom of a large flameproof casserole with leaves and arrange the rolls on top, packed tightly. Drizzle with a good pour of olive oil, then water to reach the top of the sarma. Cover and cook for 45 minutes over medium–low heat.

HANDE BOZDOĞAN

Chef and founder
of the **Istanbul Culinary Institute**

(Golden Horn)

Inspired by her chef's training at New York's French Culinary Institute, Hande Bozdoğan founded the Istanbul Culinary Institute in 2007 where young cooks learned their trade by developing the daily menu of a restaurant, **Enstitü** (in the Pera district at the time). It worked, and the restaurant had a guaranteed supply of chefs. Now that chef training is part of the syllabus of Istanbul's Kadir Has University, Hande has thrown herself into a new training project: organising workshops at her own farm to the west of Istanbul. These look at cooking from the beginning, right where it starts, as close as possible to the produce and with one's feet in the soil.

HANDE'S RECIPES
maydanoz salatası (parsley salad, page 44), Hande's kısır (Turkish tabouleh, page 62), simit kebab (veal kebabs, page 110), bulgur pilavı (burghul pilav, page 124), sarma (stuffed vine leaves, page 162), mozaik pasta (no-bake chocolate cake, page 250). Thanks to chef Bugra for his recipe for levrek güveç (sea bass stew, page 74).

ADDRESS
Chef School apprentice restaurant, *Kadir Has University, Cibali Mh., Kadir Has Caddesi, Haliç*

FLAT BEAN SALAD
ayşe kadın fasulye

Recipes are often introduced by their season in Istanbul, so it's common to hear the terms 'winter' or 'summer dish'. This is because the city's winters can be harsh and its summers hot. And so it is that there are two versions of this flat bean dish: a cold salad with olive oil for a summer appetiser and a hot dish with meat for winter.

SUMMER

Preparation time 10 minutes
Cooking time: 25 minutes
Serves 4
3 tablespoons olive oil
2 small onions, finely chopped
400 g (14 oz) Italian flat (runner) beans (fresh or frozen),
cut into 4 cm (1½ inch) lengths, or simply cut in half
3 large tomatoes, blanched, peeled and diced

Heat the olive oil in a large saucepan over medium heat. Add the onions, and sauté for about 5 minutes until soft and translucent. Add the beans, then the tomatoes. Season with salt and freshly ground black pepper, and cover. Cook over low heat (add a little water if the tomatoes are not very juicy) for about 20 minutes until the vegetables are well cooked. Serve cold.

WINTER

Preparation time: 15 minutes
Cooking time: 55 minutes
Serves 4
25 g (1 oz) butter
2 small onions, chopped
250 g (9 oz) lamb tenderloin, cut into small cubes
1 tablespoon tomato paste (concentrated purée)
2 large tomatoes, finely diced
400 g (14 oz) Italian flat (runner) beans
(fresh or frozen), cut in half
pul biber (Aleppo pepper) or other chilli flakes
(see note page 36)

Melt the butter in a large frying pan (with a lid) over medium heat. Add the onions and sauté for about 5 minutes until soft and translucent. Next, add the cubes of lamb. Once the meat has browned, add the tomato paste, tomatoes, beans and 150 ml (5 fl oz) water. Season with salt and freshly ground black pepper, cover and continue cooking for 45 minutes over low heat. Season with chilli flakes just before serving.

BÖREK

Börek, a savoury pastry made using yufka (a super-thin pastry) and filled with spinach, cheese or meat, is a dish that is also widely shared by Turkey's neighbours (Greece, Armenia, Georgia …) and up to the Balkans. It is served with morning or afternoon tea, or as a light evening meal by itself. You can find special börek yufka pastry, which is a little thicker, in Turkish or other Middle Eastern food shops or markets, and some supermarkets. You can also use very thin yufka (like filo pastry). It is up to you.

Preparation time: 45 minutes
Cooking time: 30 minutes
Serves 6–8
500 g (1 lb 2 oz) yufka pastry sheets or filo pastry sheets
250 g (9 oz) butter, melted
1 egg yolk, beaten
filling of your choice (see right)

Preheat the oven to 200°C (400°F). Separate the sheets of yufka into two equal stacks. Place the first sheet of yufka in a large, lightly oiled rectangular ovenproof dish, and brush with melted butter (do not overload it). Cover with a second sheet, brush with butter in the same way as the first one (on one side only), and repeat this process – one buttered sheet on top of another – until you have used up all of the sheets in the first stack. Spread your chosen filling over the last sheet of the stack. Cover the filling with the (buttered) sheets of the second stack, proceeding in exactly the same way as for the first half. Brush the last sheet with egg yolk, cut the börek into 8 cm (3¼ inch) squares, and bake in the oven for a good 30 minutes, or until the pastry is golden. Serve hot with lightly salted yoghurt.

WITH CHEESE

400 g (14 oz) beyaz peynir (Turkish white cheese, see page 14) or feta cheese, crumbled and mixed with 2 beaten eggs and 2 large handfuls of chopped flat-leaf (Italian) parsley or dill.

WITH SPINACH

500 g (1 lb 2 oz) baby English spinach leaves, blanched for 5 minutes in boiling water and squeezed out, mixed with 100 g (3½ oz) crumbled beyaz peynir (Turkish white cheese) or feta cheese.

WITH MEAT

500 g (1 lb 2 oz) minced (ground) meat, mixed with 1 finely chopped onion and 2 tablespoons sunflower oil, and seasoned with salt and freshly ground black pepper.

LITTLE BÖREK
FROM DELICATESSEN
Delicatessen yufka böreği

A chic little appetiser served at **Delicatessen** (see pages 130–131) in the Pera district. You can also make these as cigars, by rolling the spinach filling in a sheet of buttered yufka, brushing with egg yolk and cutting into lengths, decorated with sesame seeds.

Preparation time: 30 minutes
Cooking time: 35 minutes
Serves 2–4 (8 small börek)
10 g (¼ oz) butter, plus 20 g (¾ oz) extra, melted, for brushing
1 tablespoon olive oil
1 onion, grated
1 garlic clove, grated
300 g (10½ oz/6 cups) baby English spinach leaves
4 rectangular super-thin yufka pastry sheets (see page 168)
     or filo pastry sheets
8 chives
1 egg yolk, beaten
black sesame seeds, to decorate

Melt the 10 g (¼ oz) butter in a small frying pan with the olive oil over medium heat. Add the onion and garlic, and sauté for about 5 minutes until soft. Add the baby spinach and continue cooking for about 10 minutes. Using a sieve, gently squeeze out the moisture from the spinach. Season with salt and freshly ground black pepper, and allow the mixture to cool. Preheat the oven to 180°C (350°F). Quickly butter a sheet of the pastry with some of the extra melted butter. Place another sheet on top, butter it as well and cut – carefully, as it is fragile – into four rectangles. Place a tablespoon of the spinach mixture in the centre of each rectangle, gather up the four corners of each into a bundle and tie closed with a chive. Do the same for the rest of the rectangles, then with two other yufka sheets, which are buttered, laid on top of each other and cut into four like the previous ones. Brush the eight parcels with egg yolk, and scatter with sesame seeds. Transfer to a greased baking tray, and bake in the oven for 20 minutes.

THE YEDIKULE MARKET GARDENS

The market gardens run for 4 kilometres (2½ miles), all along the old wall of Constantinople.

STUFFED VEGETABLES
dolma

A great classic of home cooking; an eminently practical dish, with everything in it – vegetables, meat and rice – cooked together.

Preparation time: 30 minutes
Cooking time: 1 hour 30 minutes
Serves 4

1 kg (2 lb 4 oz) small capsicums (peppers) or tomatoes or small eggplants (aubergines) or zucchini (courgettes), or a mixture
200 g (7 oz) minced (ground) beef or mutton
150 g (5½ oz/⅔ cup) medium-grain rice
2 tomatoes, diced
1 onion, finely chopped
1 garlic clove, crushed
1 handful flat-leaf (Italian) parsley, finely chopped
1 handful mint, finely chopped
1 tablespoon tomato paste (concentrated purée)
200 ml (7 fl oz) olive oil

Depending on your choice of vegetable, cut off the tops of the capsicums, tomatoes or eggplants, or cut the zucchini in half lengthways. Scoop out the insides of the vegetables. Combine the meat, rice, diced tomatoes, onion, garlic, parsley, mint and tomato paste in a large bowl. Season with salt and freshly ground black pepper, and add half the olive oil. Fill the vegetables with the mixture – not completely because the rice will expand – and place them in a large flameproof casserole, resting against each other. Pour over 400 ml (14 fl oz) water and the remaining olive oil. Cover and gently cook for 1½ hours over low heat. Serve hot.

EGGPLANTS WITH MEAT
karnıyarık

Choose small eggplants if possible (or cut two large eggplants in half lengthways). No need to scoop them out; cooking them in oil beforehand will make the flesh soft and very accommodating of the filling...

Preparation time: 20 minutes
Cooking time: 30 minutes
Serves 4
4 small eggplants (aubergines)
150 ml (5 fl oz) sunflower oil
300 g (10½ oz) minced (ground) beef (you can ask your
    butcher to do this so that it is as fresh as possible)
2 long red capsicums (peppers), seeded and diced
2 bulb spring onions (scallions), finely chopped
about 24 cherry tomatoes or 3 small, ripe tomatoes,
    diced (if using cherry tomatoes, reserve about a third
    whole or halved for topping the eggplants)
1 teaspoon ground cinnamon
2 tablespoons olive oil
1 generous tablespoon tomato paste (concentrated purée)
a few flat-leaf (Italian) parsley sprigs, chopped (optional)

Wash and remove the tops of the eggplants (if you like, you can peel them in alternating strips). Heat the sunflower oil in a large frying pan over medium–high heat Add the eggplants, and fry them for 15 minutes, turning from time to time so that they brown all over; the flesh will soften. Drain on paper towel and set aside. Meanwhile, combine the meat, capsicums, spring onions, two-thirds of the tomatoes and cinnamon in a large bowl. Season with salt and freshly ground black pepper. Make an incision lengthways in the eggplants, and fill them with the stuffing. Arrange in a large saucepan (use one just snug enough that the eggplants are packed tightly against each other), and drizzle over the olive oil. Scatter over the remaining tomatoes. Mix 100–150 ml (3½–5 fl oz) water with the tomato paste and pour this mixture around the bottom of the pan. Cover and cook for 15 minutes over medium heat. Serve hot, scattered with the parsley (if using).

DIDEM ŞENOL

Chef, **Lokanta Maya** *(Karaköy)*
and **Gram** *(Beyoğlu and Sarıyer)*

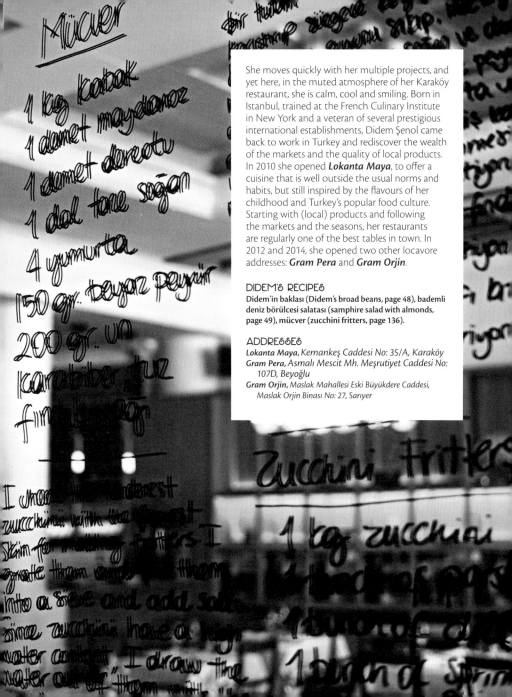

She moves quickly with her multiple projects, and yet here, in the muted atmosphere of her Karaköy restaurant, she is calm, cool and smiling. Born in Istanbul, trained at the French Culinary Institute in New York and a veteran of several prestigious international establishments, Didem Şenol came back to work in Turkey and rediscover the wealth of the markets and the quality of local products. In 2010 she opened **Lokanta Maya**, to offer a cuisine that is well outside the usual norms and habits, but still inspired by the flavours of her childhood and Turkey's popular food culture. Starting with (local) products and following the markets and the seasons, her restaurants are regularly one of the best tables in town. In 2012 and 2014, she opened two other locavore addresses: **Gram Pera** and **Gram Orjin**.

DIDEM'S RECIPES
Didem'in baklası (Didem's broad beans, page 48), bademli deniz börülcesi salatası (samphire salad with almonds, page 49), mücver (zucchini fritters, page 136).

ADDRESSES
Lokanta Maya, Kemankeş Caddesi No: 35/A, Karaköy
Gram Pera, Asmalı Mescit Mh. Meşrutiyet Caddesi No: 107D, Beyoğlu
Gram Orjin, Maslak Mahallesi Eski Büyükdere Caddesi, Maslak Orjin Binası No: 27, Sarıyer

STREET FOOD

In Turkey, street food is part of the cultural heritage. Unpretentious and, above all, very good quality, it inspires the greatest of chefs. From grilled meat or fish sandwiches to local pizzas, chestnuts, fresh juices, stuffed mussels or the little mountains of pilav rice with chickpeas sold on the city's footpaths, you can find everything on the streets and you can stop to enjoy them at any time of day. There are times for eating particular dishes, especially at night – a lahmaçun devoured at 8pm does not rule out the 2am islak burger or the 5am kokoreç. And there are places dedicated to selling these things: a street that only sells kumpir (enormous potatoes stuffed with everything) in Ortaköy; the best döner in the city at Beşiktaş, which recreates its gargantuan meat spit each morning – by afternoon, it is all gone! They will start again tomorrow…

AROUND TAKSIM
AND FURTHER NORTH

1 **Taksim Square** is the nerve centre of Istanbul. You can go everywhere from there, then come back again. To the north of the big square are hip and fashionable neighbourhoods (Nişantaşı, Bebek), ultra-modern ones, nightlife areas (Levent) and lively student neighbourhoods (Beşiktaş, Ortaköy)…

At the top of the Istiklâl Caddesi, the city's unique and unmissable pedestrian thoroughfare, **Taksim** is certainly a key intersection (a major place for demonstrations as well), but the square is equally famous for its street food and its soft islak burgers, which reach out to you from inside the
2 steamed-up glass cases that keep them warm … If you are really hungry, open the door of **Hala**, a little lower down, to try (or go back to) their mantı (dumplings) *(Büyük Parmakkapı Çukurluçeşme Sokak no: 14/A, Beyoğlu)*, or cross the Istiklâl Caddesi for the hundred and fiftieth time and arrive
3 at *Zübeyir Ocakbaşı (Şehit Muhtar Mahallesi, Bekar Sokak No: 28)*, a benchmark for kebabs – and never empty, as a matter of fact (never!). There is no off-peak period for grilled meats here.

Behind Taksim Gezi Park stretches the hip neighbourhood of Nişantaşı. There, you will find fashion and food shops side by side, luxury stores rubbing shoulders with the latest places to eat and drink; it is an embarrassment of choice. You can choose the contemporary cuisine of Elif Yalın's
4 *Delicatessen (Mim Kemal Öke Caddesi No: 19*, always such a treat) or, just next door *(No: 21)*, the
5 traditional cheerful brasserie ambience of the excellent lokanta **Hünkar**, whose reign dates from
6 1950. Four streets behind, don't go past **Kantin** *(Akkavak Sokak No: 30)*, another neighbourhood institution. Either it is lunchtime and you can run up to the dining room upstairs, or it is time for a real lemonade on the peaceful restaurant terrace. If you don't really have time for a break, go anyway to the ground floor (a shop), where you can find a good souvenir (the apple kurabiye, for example). Go back one more street and you can taste the Kürşat family's olive oils, made in Ayvalık
7 on the Aegean coast and excellent quality (**Kürşat Ayvalık Zeytinyağı**, *Şakayık Sokaka No: 75/B*).

Before you leave the neighbourhood, you must have an ice cream. To find the best of its kind, head back towards Osmanbey Station. Cross the Catholic cemetery in Feriköy and step onto
8 Kurtuluş Caddesi for a nice walk. On the right-hand footpath, you will find *Damla Doudurma Boza (Kurtuluş Caddesi No: 110/A)*: a small shop, a great artisan and irresistible ice creams that have the real flavour of fruits, caramel, chocolate … (Mastic! The best!) and an amazing stretchy consistency.

Beşiktaş is another neighbourhood to the north of Taksim in which it is worth losing yourself: a student neighbourhood and very lively, and a compulsory destination for street-food lovers.

9 If you also like sweet things, the door of *Kafadaroğlu (Ortabahçe Caddesi No: 21/G)* is open from early in the morning, a family business of master yufka pastry artisans. The home-made baklava is only in the store for a few hours. After that, it is gone – eaten. It is very, very good. Turn right and
10 take Şehit Asım Caddesi to find *7/8 Hasanpaşa Fırını (Sinanpaşa Mh., Şehit Asım Caddesi No: 12)*. Behind the small counter of this bakery is a huge room with mountains of kurabiye and various breads, all very inviting. If you are more in the mood for a good sandwich … well, you are in the right place. There is no lack of them in this neighbourhood. You will find an excellent lahmaçun by going
11 back down Mumcu Bakkal Sokak, then turning right (Kazan Sokak), at *Abusta 33 Mersin Tantuni (Sinanpaşa Mahallesi Kazan Sokak No: 7/B)*.

12 A couple of steps from there is the famous *Karadeniz Döner* – supposedly the best döner kebab in the city – with its eno-o-o-ormous vertical spit that is remade every morning. At the end of the afternoon, the shop closes; there is nothing left. Baklava, döner – it is all the same.

13 On Saturdays, do not miss the **covered market in Beşiktaş** (Nüzhetiye Caddesi), which has everything going for it: fresh, abundant, varied produce, colours everywhere, mounds of spices, rice, nuts and cakes, and spotless, well-ordered stalls. The men carrying big baskets even offer you their services (carrying your shopping). And all of that lit up by scores (hundreds?) of hanging light bulbs that give this unpretentious and lively market a festive air.

To the north of Beşiktaş (take Çirağan Caddesi, going back up the Bosphorus), the district
14 of **Ortaköy** has dedicated one of its streets to kumpir, potatoes stuffed with everything you could want. It is as if the vendors, side by side, are in a competition for who can add the most filling. The question is: Where on earth do these giant potatoes come from in the first place?

Off the map: the neighbourhood of Emirgan

To pursue your travels and take the time to see the city from the strait, head up the Bosphorus to the neighbourhood of Emirgan (beyond the second bridge, the boats stop there), cross the street and enter the **Sakıp Sabancı Müzesi** (*Emirgan Mahallesi, Sakıp Sabancı Caddesi No: 42*). Breathe in the fresh air of its pretty garden and enter to admire its permanent collection dedicated to calligraphy, or whatever temporary exhibition of modern painting that is showing at the time. After all this mad activity, sit yourself down at the museum restaurant, *Müzedechanga* (the little brother of the very famous *Changa*, a couple of steps from Taksim and a pioneer of Istanbul's new cuisine). Enjoy the divine terrace that looks over the water and an astonishing menu that reinvents Turkish cuisine. Your plate will be as beautiful as it is delicious. A place of subtle combinations that suits Istanbul well.

ISLAK BURGER

You can find these little burgers, doused in a garlicky tomato sauce, day and night in Taksim Square, waiting in their Turkish bath for a passing reveller to sate their ravishing hunger. Some add a touch of mild or hot biber salçası (Turkish chilli paste, see page 34) to the mix.

Preparation time: 15 minutes
Cooking time: 15–20 minutes
Makes 4 hamburgers
3 garlic cloves
150 ml (5 fl oz) tomato passata (puréed tomatoes)
2 tablespoons olive oil
400 g (14 oz) minced (ground) beef (ask your butcher
    to do this so that it is as fresh as possible)
4 round hamburger buns, split in half through
    the middle and lightly buttered

Crush the garlic with a little salt using a mortar and pestle. Mix together the tomato passata, 1 tablespoon of the olive oil and the garlic in a large bowl. Season with freshly ground black pepper. Set aside. Divide the meat into four equal portions, and shape into four patties. In a large frying pan over medium–high heat, sear the patties quickly on both sides (about 1 minute) in the remaining oil. Pour over the tomato sauce, reduce the heat to very, very low and cook for 5 minutes; the meat needs to become impregnated with the sauce. Push the patties to one side of the frying pan, and arrange the bun halves face down on the tomato sauce. Cover and cook for 10 minutes (still over low heat). The buns should be 'wet' – that is the whole idea. To finish, sandwich each patty between two pieces of bun.

TURKISH PIZZA
lahmaçun

The flavours of Istanbul can also be found in Rue du Faubourg-Saint-Denis in my own city, Paris. Thank you to Samuel Yafamis and the chef at **Istanbul** for initiating me into the preparation of lahmaçun and pide.

Preparation time: 10 minutes
Resting time: 1 hour
Cooking time: 5–10 minutes
Makes 4 small pizzas

DOUGH
2 g (¹⁄₁₆ oz) fresh yeast or ½ teaspoon dried
200 g (7 oz/1⅓ cups) strong flour

TOPPING
140 g (5 oz) minced (ground) beef mixed with
    60 g (2¼ oz) minced (ground) lamb shoulder
1 small onion, finely chopped
1 long green capsicum (pepper), seeded and finely chopped
2 ripe tomatoes, finely chopped
pul biber (Aleppo pepper) or other chilli flakes
    (see note page 36)

First, make the dough. Combine the yeast with 150 ml (5 fl oz) lukewarm water in a small bowl until it has completely dissolved. Sift the flour into a large bowl, and add a large pinch of salt. Make a well in the centre, and gradually mix in the yeast mixture, drawing in flour from the sides, until the dough comes together; knead on a lightly floured surface, to make a ball of smooth, elastic dough. Put in a lightly oiled bowl, and cover with a damp tea towel (dish towel). Leave to rest in a warm, draught-free place for at least 1 hour, or until doubled in size. To make the topping, put the meat, onion, capsicum and tomatoes in a large bowl, and mix through evenly. Add a sprinkle of chilli flakes to taste, and season with salt and freshly ground black pepper. Preheat the oven to 180°C (350°F). After the proving time, knead the dough until smooth and elastic once again, and divide into four equal portions. Roll out each one into a thin, slightly oval shape (like a flatbread) on a lightly floured work surface, and top all over with the spiced meat mixture. Bake for 5–10 minutes until crisp and golden.

PIDE

Pide are a sort of boat-shaped pizza, cooked in a wood-fired oven. Here they are made with cheese, English spinach or chicken, but you can also fill them with minced beef, pieces of mutton, or sucuk (spicy cured sausage), with an egg on top of the meat and a tomato-parsley-capsicum mixture, as shown in the picture.

Preparation time: 10 minutes
Resting time: 1 hour
Cooking time: 10–12 minutes
Makes 1 pide
**6 g (⅛ oz/2 teaspoons) fresh yeast
or 1 teaspoon dried
90 ml (3 fl oz) lukewarm water
100 g (3½ oz/⅔ cup) strong flour**

To make the dough, combine the yeast with the lukewarm water in a small bowl until it has completely dissolved. Sift the flour into a bowl, and add a big pinch of salt. Make a well in the centre, and gradually mix in the yeast mixture, drawing in flour from the sides, until the dough comes together; knead on a lightly floured surface, to make a ball of smooth, elastic dough. Put in a lightly oiled bowl, and cover with a damp tea towel (dish towel). Leave to rest in a warm, draught-free place for at least 1 hour, or until doubled in size.

WITH CHEESE

kaşarlı pide
**1 portion of dough (see above)
100–150 g (3½–5½ oz) beyaz peynir (Turkish white
cheese, see page 14) or feta cheese, crumbled
1 long green chilli
2 tomato slices
1 egg
pul biber (Aleppo pepper) or other chilli flakes
(see note page 36)**

Preheat the oven to 180°C (350°F). Once the dough has rested, knead until smooth and elastic once again, before rolling it out on a floured work surface into the (pretty) shape of the hull of a ship, about 40 cm (16 inches) long and 15 cm (6 inches) wide. Top with the cheese (leave a border), place the chilli in the middle with the tomato slices either side and season with salt. Fold over the long sides of the dough about 2 cm (¾ inch) towards the middle, then the ends, to hold the ingredients in the 'hull'. Break the egg on top, and bake for 10–12 minutes. Season with chilli flakes.

WITH SPINACH

ispanakli pide
**1 portion of dough (see left)
2 handfuls baby English spinach leaves
½ onion, sliced into rings
130 g (4½ oz) beyaz peynir (Turkish white cheese,
see page 14) or feta cheese, crumbled**

Preheat the oven to 180°C (350°F). Once the dough has rested, knead until smooth and elastic once again, before rolling it out on a floured work surface into the shape of a ship's hull, about 40 cm (16 inches) long and 20 cm (8 inches) wide (a bit wider than for standard pide). Lay the spinach, onion and crumbled cheese all along the length of the pide (leave a border), season with salt and fold the dough over the filling completely, pressing the edges together well with your fingers. Bake for 10–12 minutes.

WITH CHICKEN

tavuklu pide
**1 portion dough (see above left)
100 g (3½ oz) minced (ground) free-range skinless
chicken breast fillet
1 small long red or green capsicum (pepper),
seeded and diced
1 large tomato, diced
a few flat-leaf (Italian) parsley sprigs, chopped**

Preheat the oven to 180°C (350°F). Once the dough has rested, knead until smooth and elastic once again, before rolling it out on a floured work surface into the (pretty) shape of a ship's hull, about 40 cm (16 inches) long and 15 cm (6 inches) wide. Top with the chicken, capsicum and tomato, and sprinkle with the parsley. Season with salt and freshly ground black pepper, then fold over the long sides of the dough about 2 cm (¾ inch) towards the middle, then the ends, to hold the ingredients in the 'hull'. Bake for 10–12 minutes.

FISH SANDWICH
balık ekmek

'Balık' is fish and 'ekmek' is bread. A simple combination, but the two work very well together. You can find this sandwich by the water's edge in Istanbul – next to Karaköy's fish market at the feet of the Galata bridge, for example. The best are seasoned with an in-house spice mix; if you do not make one yourself, you can find special ready-made spice mixes for fish easily enough.

Preparation time: 5 minutes
Cooking time: 10 minutes
Makes 1 sandwich
1 mackerel fillet, cleaned
a little olive oil
⅓ baguette
salad of chopped lettuce, sliced onion, diced tomato and
     seeded and diced long red capsicum (pepper)
pomegranate molasses (available from Turkish or other Middle Eastern
     food shops, some supermarkets and online) or lemon juice
pul biber (Aleppo pepper) or other chilli flakes
     (see note page 36)
fish spices of your choice

Season the fish fillet with salt, and grill it on a hot barbecue for a couple of minutes on each side, or pan-fry in a little olive oil in a medium frying pan over high heat for 1–2 minutes longer. Meanwhile, slice the baguette in half lengthways (without cutting all the way through), open up and place on top of the fish on the grill or in the pan for a short minute to toast lightly and absorb the flavour of the fish. Remove from the grill or pan. Fill the baguette with the salad, then top with the mackerel fillet. Dress with a drizzle of pomegranate molasses, a scattering of chilli flakes and fish spices to taste. Serve hot.

STUFFED POTATOES
kumpir

In Istanbul, the kumpir potatoes are giant (huge!), the fillings are excessive and you wonder how you will ever get to the end (by yourself) of this very good sort of mashed potato sandwich.

Preparation time: 10 minutes
Cooking time: 45 minutes
Makes 1 kumpir

1 very large roasting potato such as russet (idaho), king edward, bintje (yellow finn) or similar
25 g (1 oz) butter
Filling is … whatever you like: diced tomato, corn, sliced mushrooms, sliced olives, 1 chopped bulb spring onion (scallion), 1 grated carrot or some red cabbage, pickled vegetables (gherkins) …
40 g (1½ oz) kaşar or gruyère or mozzarella cheese, grated
sauces: mayonnaise, ketchup, cacık …

Preheat the oven to 200°C (400°F). Scrub the potato with a brush, pat dry with paper towel and prick with a fork in about six places all over. Bake in the oven for about 45 minutes (more or less depending on its size), wrapped in a foil parcel. To check whether it is done, insert a knife into the flesh – it is cooked when it is very soft. Open up the potato lengthways like a book (but without dividing it into two halves). Melt the butter in the middle of the potato by mixing it into the flesh with a spoon or fork. Fill the potato with whatever you like and finish with the grated cheese and your choice of sauce. Serve hot.

OUTSIDE OF ISTANBUL, YOU WONDER WHERE YOU CAN FIND SUCH GIANT POTATOES.

TRIPE SANDWICH
kokoreç

Another classic of Istanbul night-time menus.

Preparation time: 10 minutes
Cooking time: 10–15 minutes
Makes 1 sandwich
100 g (3½ oz) pre-cooked tripe,
    finely diced (see page 88)
sunflower oil
2 small long red capsicums (peppers),
    seeded and finely diced
⅓ baguette
1 tablespoon dried thyme
pul biber (Aleppo pepper) or other
    chilli flakes (see note page 36)
chilli-flavoured olive oil

Drizzle the tripe with some sunflower oil,
and sauté on the grill or in a frying pan over
medium–high heat for about 15 minutes.
Add the capsicums to the tripe towards the
end of the cooking time, to soften, then open
up the baguette lengthways and fill with this
mixture. Season with the thyme and chilli
flakes, chilli oil and salt to taste. Serve hot.

STUFFED MUSSELS
midye dolma

This cold hors d'œuvre, ideally made the day before, is a classic. In Beşiktas, a student neighbourhood and an El Dorado for lovers of street food, you can eat stuffed mussels, size XXL, all day long, sold by the piece and served with lemon wedges.

Preparation time: 40 minutes
Soaking time: 20 minutes
Cooking time: 30 minutes
Resting time: at least 6 hours
Serves 4

20–30 large fresh mussels
150 ml (5 fl oz) sunflower oil
800 g (1 lb 12 oz) onions, finely chopped
100 g (3½ oz/⅔ cup) pine nuts
170 g (6 oz/generous ¾ cup) medium-grain rice
1 tablespoon ground cinnamon
1 teaspoon ground allspice
1 lemon, cut into wedges

Clean the mussels (without removing their beards), and soak them for about 20 minutes in a large container of fresh cold water; discard any broken mussels, or open ones that do not close when tapped on the work surface. Rinse several times while soaking, swirling the mussels around and refilling with fresh cold water. Meanwhile, heat the sunflower oil in a medium to large frying pan over medium heat. Add the onions and pine nuts, and sauté for 10 minutes, or until the onions are soft and the pine nuts are golden. Add the rice, cinnamon and allspice; season with salt, mix, then turn off the heat and allow to cool. Open the mussels with a knife, being careful not to break or separate the shells. Cut through the muscle at the side of the shell, and remove the beard. Fill the mussels with the rice mixture, arrange them side by side in a large lidded saucepan, and add two generous ladlefuls of water (you want the mussels to steam in the pan). Cover with the lid, and bring the water to a very gentle simmer over medium heat. Reduce the heat to low and cook, covered, for about 20 minutes. Let the mussels cool completely, and leave the dish to rest in the refrigerator for several hours, or even a day or two. Serve with lemon wedges for squeezing over.

WRAPS
dürüm

A dürüm is a thin unleavened flatbread that can be filled with anything you like – meats and vegetables of all kinds – to create a wonderful rolled sandwich.

Preparation time: 10 minutes
Resting time: at least 1 hour
Cooking time: 10 minutes
Makes 1 wrap

DOUGH
100 g (3½ oz/⅔ cup) strong flour
90 ml (3 fl oz) lukewarm water

SALAD
chopped lettuce
red onion slices
rocket (arugula)
flat-leaf (Italian) parsley
tomato slices seasoned with salt, sumac and pul
 biber (Aleppo pepper) or other chilli flakes

To make the dough, combine the flour, a good pinch of salt and the water in a small bowl until they come together, then knead for a few minutes to make a ball of smooth, elastic dough. Leave to rest in a lightly oiled bowl for at least 1 hour (the dough is better made the day before). Make the filling of your choice (see right). On a lightly floured work surface, roll out the dough very thinly in the shape of a round flatbread. Lay the flatbread in a very hot frying pan (without adding any fat), cooking for 30 seconds on each side. Place the salad, then your choice of filling in the middle of the flatbread, season with salt, sumac and chilli flakes to taste, and roll the bread into a cylinder. Serve hot.

LAMB

100 g (3½ oz) lamb tenderloin, cut into cubes and
 marinated in 1 teaspoon tatlı biber salçası
 (mild Turkish chilli paste, see page 34),
 a little sunflower oil and salt
OR trimmed and cleaned lamb's liver, diced and seasoned

Thread the cubes of meat onto skewers (if using wooden skewers, soak them in cold water beforehand). Grill on a medium-hot barbecue (or under a preheated grill/broiler or in a frying pan), turning, until cooked through.

MINCED MEATS

100 g (3½ oz) minced (ground) beef
60 g (2 oz) minced (ground) lamb shoulder
1 small garlic clove
a little finely chopped onion
chopped flat-leaf (Italian) parsley

Mix together all of the ingredients, and season with salt. Shape the meat onto skewers (if using wooden skewers, soak them in cold water beforehand). Grill on a medium-hot barbecue (or under a preheated medium-hot grill/broiler or in a frying pan), turning, until cooked through.

CHICKEN

100 g (3½ oz) free-range skinless chicken
 thigh fillet, cut into cubes
1 small garlic clove, crushed
½ teaspoon ground cumin
sunflower oil

Mix together the chicken, garlic and cumin in a bowl. Drizzle with a little sunflower oil, and season with salt. Thread the cubes of chicken onto skewers (if using wooden skewers, soak them in cold water beforehand). Grill on a medium-hot barbecue (or under a preheated grill/broiler or in a frying pan), turning, until cooked through.

YOGHURT

Yoghurt is a central and essential ingredient of Turkish food. Turkey is where it was invented a very long time ago – the first references to 'yoğurt' date from a thousand years ago. Since then, its use has spread all around the world. Turkish or Greek-style yoghurt, which you can find in large tubs in Middle Eastern food shops and even some supermarkets, can be made from sheep's or goat's milk, but most often from cow's milk. It is thicker and creamier than the standard tub of plain yoghurt familiar from my French childhood (and the school cafeteria!). A symbol of Turkish gastronomy, yoghurt is associated with savoury dishes and is very often served with meals: in the form of a drink, hot sauce or cold dressing for a meat or pastry dish, or just as is in the form of a soup or meze, to quell the fire of a spice or just because it is good for the digestion ...

AYRAN

Cold ayran, a traditional drink of salted yoghurt, is often served with meats, especially spicy meats.

Preparation time: 5 minutes
Serves 1
130 g (4½ oz/½ cup) Turkish or Greek-style yoghurt
½ teaspoon salt

Chill a small glass of water with ice cubes (or in the freezer) for a few minutes. Pour the yoghurt into a bowl, salt lightly and add a little of the iced water (about 150 ml/5 fl oz, more or less, depending on the consistency you prefer), until the yoghurt is liquid but still creamy.

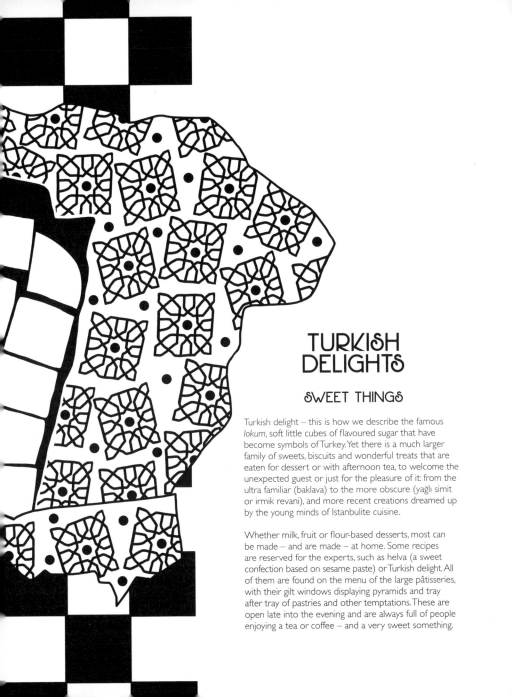

TURKISH DELIGHTS

SWEET THINGS

Turkish delight – this is how we describe the famous *lokum*, soft little cubes of flavoured sugar that have become symbols of Turkey. Yet there is a much larger family of sweets, biscuits and wonderful treats that are eaten for dessert or with afternoon tea, to welcome the unexpected guest or just for the pleasure of it: from the ultra familiar (baklava) to the more obscure (yağlı simit or irmik revani), and more recent creations dreamed up by the young minds of Istanbulite cuisine.

Whether milk, fruit or flour-based desserts, most can be made – and are made – at home. Some recipes are reserved for the experts, such as helva (a sweet confection based on sesame paste) or Turkish delight. All of them are found on the menu of the large pâtisseries, with their gilt windows displaying pyramids and tray after tray of pastries and other temptations. These are open late into the evening and are always full of people enjoying a tea or coffee – and a very sweet something.

MAKING BAKLAVA

BAKLAVA

Baklava is usually bought from specialists, of course. This sweet little pastry makes a good present, but is equally enjoyable if you feel like treating yourself at home.

Preparation time: 45 minutes
Cooking time: 35 minutes
Makes about 60 baklava
500 g (1 lb 2 oz) yufka pastry
sheets (see page 168)
or filo pastry sheets
250 g (9 oz) butter, melted

250 g (9 oz) unsalted pistachio
nut kernels or walnuts,
crushed or ground
1 tablespoon ground cinnamon
SYRUP (ABOUT 400 ML/14 FL OZ)
400 g (14 oz/generous 1¾ cups)
caster (superfine) sugar
1 tablespoon lemon juice

First, make the syrup. Put the sugar and 200 ml (7 fl oz) water in a small saucepan, and stir until the sugar has dissolved. Place the saucepan over medium heat. Bring to the boil, still stirring, and skim off any white froth that forms on the surface. Add the lemon juice and continue to cook, stirring, for a further 3 minutes. Set aside to cool. Mix together the nuts and cinnamon. Preheat the oven to 180°C (350°F). Brush a pastry sheet with melted butter (on one side only and without overdoing it). Carefully cover with another sheet, brush it on top with butter as well, and repeat this process until you have five sheets layered on top of each other. Sprinkle with the cinnamon-flavoured nuts, cut the pile of pastry sheets down the middle and roll each half into a (fairly tight) long cigar. Place these rolls in a large ovenproof dish, and repeat until you have run out of pastry sheets and butter – keep a handful of nuts in reserve to decorate the top of the pastry. You should have about 10 rolls packed together. Cut each one carefully into six parts, to make baklava about 5 cm (2 inches) long. Scatter over the rest of the nuts. Bake in the oven for 30 minutes until golden brown. When they come out of the oven, pour over the cold syrup.

Another method: Butter the top side of each sheet of yufka and arrange half the pastry sheets in a large rectangular tin, one on top of the other, but without packing them down. Arrange the nuts on this first set of sheets (keeping back a handful for the top of the baklava), and cover with the second half of buttered pastry sheets. Cut into 3 cm (1¼ inch) wide strips, then into 5 cm (2 inch) long rectangles, and sprinkle with the rest of the nuts. Bake in the oven for 30 minutes. When the baklava comes out of the oven, pour over the cold syrup.

CHEESE PASTRY
künefe

You can find this pastry, made from kadayif (angel hair pastry) and cheese, from the Middle East to Greece. The Turks use a desalted cheese; mozzarella does the job very well.

Preparation time: 25 minutes
Cooking time: 20 minutes
Serves 6
250 g (9 oz/½ packet) kadayif (angel hair) pastry (available from Turkish, other Middle Eastern and Mediterranean food shops)
250 g (9 oz) fresh mozzarella cheese, torn into pieces
125 g (4½ oz) butter, melted and cooled until lukewarm
kaymak (buffalo's milk clotted cream) or mascarpone cheese, to serve
SYRUP (ABOUT 200 ML/7 FL OZ)
200 g (7 oz/scant 1 cup) caster (superfine) sugar
1 tablespoon lemon juice

First, make the syrup. Put the sugar and 125 ml (4 fl oz/½ cup) water in a small saucepan, and stir until the sugar has dissolved. Place the saucepan over medium heat. Bring the syrup mixture to the boil, still stirring, and skim off any white froth that forms on the surface. Add the lemon juice and continue to cook, stirring, for a further 3 minutes. Set aside to cool. Untangle and cut the angel hair pastry with scissors (into short 1–2 cm/½–¾ inch lengths) into a large bowl, then mix with the lukewarm melted butter, making sure that you take the time to work the butter through the pastry evenly. Separate into two equal portions. Spread the first portion of pastry over the bottom of a medium frying pan, cover with the mozzarella and top with the second half of the pastry. Pan-fry over medium heat for 10 minutes, or until the pastry is golden underneath. Turn over and cook on the other side (use a plate to carefully slide out and invert the künefe) for a further 10 minutes. Pour the cold syrup over the künefe and serve hot, cut into wedges or squares, with some kaymak.

Note: Kaymak is a Turkish dairy product usually made from buffalo's milk. The milk and/or cream is cooked over very low heat, then left to cool and slightly ferment until thickened. It is similar in many ways to clotted cream and crème fraîche, and either of these can be used as a substitute (as well as mascarpone cheese) if kaymak is unavailable where you live.

PISTACHIO KADAYIF

A cousin of the künefe (cheese pastry) on the previous page, this angel hair pastry is served cold.

Preparation time: 25 minutes
Cooking time: 35 minutes
Resting time: 4 hours
Serves 6
250 g (9 oz) kadayif (angel hair) pastry (available from Turkish, other Middle Eastern and Mediterranean food shops)
125 g (4½ oz) butter, melted and cooled until lukewarm
150 g (5½ oz) unsalted pistachio nut kernels, ground (not too coarsely and not too fine)
SYRUP (ABOUT 200 ML/7 FL OZ)
200 g (7 oz/scant 1 cup) caster (superfine) sugar
1 tablespoon lemon juice

First, make the syrup. Put the sugar and 125 ml (4 fl oz/½ cup) water in a small saucepan, and stir until the sugar has dissolved. Place the saucepan over medium heat. Bring the syrup mixture to the boil, still stirring, and skim off any white froth that forms on the surface. Add the lemon juice and continue to cook, stirring, for a further 3 minutes. Set aside to cool. Preheat the oven to 180°C (350°F). Untangle and cut the angel hair pastry with scissors (into short 1–2 cm/½–¾ inch lengths) into a large bowl, then mix with the lukewarm melted butter, making sure that you take the time to work it through the pastry evenly. Separate the pastry into two equal portions. Spread the first half over the bottom of a rectangular baking tin (about 30 x 20 cm/12 x 8 inches). Spread the nuts evenly over the first layer of pastry. Top with the other portion of pastry, and bake in the oven for 30 minutes, or until the kadayif is golden brown. Pour the cold syrup over the hot pastry while it is still in the tin. Allow to cool for 4 hours at room temperature before serving.

VANILLA MILK PUDDING
muhallebi

Muhallebi can also be flavoured with orange flower water or rosewater: if you want to try that, replace the vanilla with 60 ml (2 fl oz/¼ cup) of either water, and add to the pudding when it starts to thicken.

Preparation time: 5 minutes
Cooking time: 10 minutes
Resting time: 4 hours
Serves 4
30 g (1 oz/¼ cup) cornflour (cornstarch)
500 ml (17 fl oz/2 cups) milk
90 g (3¼ oz/generous ⅓ cup) caster (superfine) sugar
1 vanilla bean
1 small handful crushed unsalted pistachio nut kernels

Blend the cornflour into a little of the milk, add this mixture to the rest of the milk in a saucepan with the sugar, and stir to dissolve. Open the vanilla bean lengthways, and scrape out the seeds over the saucepan, then add the bean to the milk. Gently heat over medium heat, stirring constantly, for about 10 minutes until the mixture thickens. Pour into four small individual ramekins, and decorate the top of each one with a generous pinch of crushed nuts. Once the puddings have cooled, set aside the ramekins in the refrigerator for several hours to chill until ready to serve.

CRÈME BRÛLÉE
kazandibi

The custard of the kazandibi, which is fairly solid,
is cut into squares and eaten like a cake.

Preparation time: 20 minutes
Cooking time: 30 minutes
Resting time: 4 hours
Serves 8

500 ml (17 fl oz/2 cups) milk
200 ml (7 fl oz) thin (pouring) cream
50 g (1¾ oz/scant ½ cup) cornflour (cornstarch)
110 g (4 oz/½ cup) caster (superfine) sugar
piece of mastic gum (about the size of half a sugar cube), ground
**   to a powder using a mortar and pestle (see note)**
ground cinnamon or crushed unsalted pistachio nut kernels, to decorate

CARAMEL
40 g (1½ oz) butter
3 tablespoons caster (superfine) sugar

In a large saucepan, stir together the milk, cream, cornflour, sugar and mastic.
Place the saucepan over medium heat, and stir with a whisk or a wooden
spoon for about 10 minutes until the mixture has taken on a very thick
consistency. Turn off the heat and set aside. To make the caramel, preheat
the oven from the bottom to 250°C (500°F). Spread the butter over the
bottom of a medium–large ovenproof dish and sprinkle with the sugar.
Pour over the custard, and cook in the oven for 15–20 minutes until
the sugar has caramelised at the bottom of the dish. Chill in the refrigerator
for 4 hours. Serve cold, cut into squares and sprinkled with the cinnamon
or nuts.

Another option: lightly butter a 25 cm (10 inch) round or 30 x 20 cm
(12 x 8 inch) rectangular baking tin. Carefully pour in the custard. Sprinkle
the top with the sugar (or with the melted butter and sugar mixture),
and brown under a preheated hot grill (broiler) for 10 minutes (keeping
watch over it to make sure that the sugar does not catch and burn).

Note: Mastic gum is derived from the sap of the mastic tree. It is also
known as Arabic Gum (not to be confused with 'gum arabic') and Tears
of Chios. It can be purchased online and at some health-food stores.

CHOUX FRITTERS IN SYRUP
tulumba

Very good little fritters that are at their best when freshly cooked. This version is not as sweet as the ones sold on the streets of Istanbul, which ooze with syrup.

Preparation time: 10 minutes
Cooking time: 30 minutes
Serves 4

DOUGH
40 g (1½ oz) butter
200 g (7 oz/1⅓ cups) plain (all-purpose) flour
3 eggs
sunflower or other vegetable oil for deep-frying

SYRUP (ABOUT 300 ML/10½ FL OZ)
300 g (10½ oz/generous 1⅓ cups) caster (superfine) sugar
1 tablespoon lemon juice

First, make the syrup. Put the sugar and 300 ml (10½ fl oz) water in a small saucepan, and stir until the sugar has dissolved. Place the saucepan over low heat. Bring to the boil, still stirring, and skim off any white froth that forms on the surface. Add the lemon juice and continue to cook, stirring, for a further 3 minutes. Set aside to cool. Melt the butter in 300 ml (10½ fl oz) salted water in a medium saucepan over medium heat, then add the flour all at once and mix with a wooden spoon until the dough comes away from the side and bottom of the pan. Add the eggs, one by one, mixing well after each addition. In a deep, heavy-based saucepan, heat enough oil for deep-frying until it reaches 180°C (350°F), or until a cube of bread turns golden brown in 15 seconds; keep the heat even throughout the frying process. Put the fritter batter in a piping (icing) bag with a 1–1.5 cm (½–⅝ inch) fluted nozzle. Pipe out lengths a few centimetres long, snipping them off with scissors, and carefully add to the oil. Work in batches if needed, so that you do not crowd the pan. Deep-fry the fritters for a couple of minutes until crisp and golden all over, before carefully removing from the pan with a slotted spoon. Drain on a plate lined with paper towel. Once all the fritters are cooked, transfer to a serving dish and pour the cold syrup over the top.

SHORTBREADS
kurabiye

Ah! Kurabiye. The piles of little biscuits, snowy with icing sugar, that beckon seductively at passersby from the windows of the bakeries! You could stop to eat them everywhere. In a legendary fırın in Beşiktas, in a chic café in Nişantaşı, in a discreet little shop in Cihangir … They come in various shapes and flavours: plain, with apple, walnuts, almonds …

Preparation time: 20 minutes
Resting time: 30 minutes
Cooking time: 25 minutes
Makes about 25 shortbreads
400 g (14 oz/2⅔ cups) plain (all-purpose) flour
1 teaspoon baking powder
80 g (2¾ oz/⅓ cup) caster (superfine) sugar
pinch of pure vanilla powder
100 g (3½ oz/1 cup) ground almonds or walnuts
250 g (9 oz) butter, diced and softened
100 ml (3½ fl oz) milk
icing (confectioners') sugar for dusting

Combine the flour, baking powder, caster sugar, vanilla, ground almonds and diced butter in a large bowl, and work with your fingertips until you have an even mixture the texture of breadcrumbs. Add the milk, and shape into a ball. Leave the dough to rest at room temperature for 30 minutes. Preheat the oven to 180°C (350°F). Quickly knead the dough on a floured work surface for 1 minute. Remove pieces of dough the size of a plum (about 40 g/1½ oz each), shape into small balls and flatten each one slightly. Arrange on a baking tray covered with baking paper, and cook in the oven for about 25 minutes. Dust generously with icing sugar when they come out of the oven.

A GOOD VARIATION USING THE SAME DOUGH: APPLE FILLING
(Allow 1 apple for 3 biscuits.) Peel, core and grate the apples. Mix with a good handful of currants and sprinkle with ground cinnamon. Flatten a small ball (40 g/1½ oz) of dough into a circle about 10 cm (4 inches) in diameter. Put a little of the spiced apple on one half of each round of dough (leaving a border around the edge), and fold over to form a half-circle; press the edges together with your fingertips. Bake in a preheated 180°C (350°F) oven for 25 minutes, then dust generously with icing sugar.

SAVOURY SESAME BISCUITS
yağlı simit

It is easy to become dependent on these savoury biscuits (crackers): alongside the five o'clock coffee, or afterwards with drinks (in which case, make smaller biscuits), or perhaps before – or basically all through the day for me because yağlı simit are extremely good. 'Yağlı' means 'fat', and the tag comes from the fact that this biscuit contains fat, unlike the standard simit (leavened bread) that you find in Istanbul's streets.

Preparation time: 15 minutes
Resting time: 30 minutes
Cooking time: 30 minutes
Makes about 12 biscuits
100 g (3½ oz) butter
2 tablespoons Turkish or Greek-style yoghurt
125 ml (4 fl oz/½ cup) sunflower oil
1 teaspoon baking powder
1 teaspoon caster (superfine) sugar
½ teaspoon salt
300 g (10½ oz/2 cups) plain (all-purpose) flour

TO FINISH
1 egg yolk mixed with a few drops of olive oil
**2 tablespoons white or black sesame seeds, or a
   mixture of both (about 20 g/¾ oz in total)**

Melt the butter in a small saucepan over low heat. Mix together with all the other ingredients except the flour; add this last and continue mixing until the mixture comes together. Leave to rest for 30 minutes. Preheat the oven to 180°C (350°F). Take small pieces of dough (about 40 g/1½ oz each), and roll into sausages about 15 cm (6 inches) long. Shape them into rings by joining the two ends, overlapping them slightly. Brush the tops of the biscuits with the egg yolk mixed with olive oil (to make them shine!), then dip them in the mixed sesame seeds. Bake in the oven for 30 minutes.

MAKING LOKUM

MASTIC TURKISH DELIGHT
sakızlı lokum

Turkish delight is not easy to get right. The secret lies in the soft texture of the sweet and thus in the cooking of the sugar. If not cooked enough, it will stay too soft; too long on the heat and it will harden as it cools. As a result, you need to watch the consistency of the sugar paste very carefully during cooking; before taking it off the heat, it should be like a dense, malleable rubber.

Preparation time: 5 minutes
Cooking time: 30 minutes
For a few handfuls of Turkish delight
20 g (¾ oz) cornflour (cornstarch)
200 g (7 oz/scant 1 cup) caster (superfine) sugar
1 tablespoon lemon juice
2 g (¹⁄₁₆ oz) piece mastic gum (about
5 mm/¼ inch in diameter), ground to
a powder using a mortar and pestle
(see note page 222)
icing (confectioners') sugar for dusting

Variation: You can flavour the Turkish delight with (200 ml/7 fl oz) pomegranate juice or orange flower water instead of water, or add (50 g/1¾ oz) sweetened fruit purée or (20 g/¾ oz) roughly chopped almonds or pistachio nut kernels) to the mixture after the lemon juice.

Prepare a small heatproof glass or ceramic dish (about 16 x 10 x 6 cm/6 x 4 x 2 inches) for the Turkish delight: it needs to be narrow (the cubes of Turkish delight will be a good 2 cm/¾ inch tall and wide), and very lightly greased with a few drops of sunflower oil, then coated with cornflour (cornstarch). Pour 150 ml (5 fl oz) water into a glass. Take 3 tablespoons of it and blend with the cornflour to make a paste. Add the rest with the sugar in a medium saucepan, and stir off the heat until completely dissolved. Next, stir the cornflour paste into the sugar syrup. Place the saucepan over medium heat, and gently stir for about 10 minutes. When the sugar comes to the boil, reduce the heat slightly (between medium and low), add the lemon juice and mastic, and continue to cook, stirring regularly. After a good further 20 minutes, the sugar will take on the consistency of a thick gum that sticks to the spoon, comes away cleanly from the sides of the pan and takes time to sink back to the bottom. Pour the mixture into the prepared dish, and leave to cool. Dust with icing sugar, and cut into small cubes.

IT IS TRUE THAT ISTANBULITES BUY TURKISH DELIGHT RATHER THAN MAKE IT. BUT IF YOU CANNOT BE THERE, YOU CAN ALWAYS PRETEND A LITTLE WITH THIS RECIPE.

ŞEKERCİ

Aytekin Erol

CAFERZADE

www.caferzade.com.tr

OSMANLIDAN
DAMAK TADI

ÖZEL YAPIM
SADE
LOKUM

14.00 ₺

ALM⊘ND HELVA
badem helvası

Well worth the trouble of making, this sesame–almond paste is a simple and delicious treat.

Preparation time: 10 minutes
Cooking time: 5 minutes
Resting time: overnight
For lots of friends
150 g (5½ oz/⅔ cup) caster (superfine) sugar
125 g (4½ oz/⅔ cup) fine semolina
65 g (2¼ oz/¼ cup) tahini
50 g (1¾ oz/½ cup) ground almonds

Put the sugar and 60 ml (2 fl oz/¼ cup) water in a medium, heavy-based saucepan, and stir until the sugar has dissolved. Place over medium heat, and cook the syrup until it reaches 115°C (240°F; soft-ball stage) – if you do not have a sugar (candy) thermometer, wait (not long) until the boiling bubbles become larger. Turn off the heat, and add the semolina, then incorporate the tahini and ground almonds, and mix to a smooth paste. Spread out the paste in a small dish (the helva should be a good 3 cm/1¼ inches deep), allow it to cool and set aside in the refrigerator to chill overnight. Cut into slices or small squares for serving.

FL☺UR HELVA
un helvası

Helva is sold by specialists because it can be a little tricky to make at home (it needs to be stirred constantly, but covered at the same time). There are many variations, and this flour-based helva is Nurdane's favourite – it was Nurdane who gave me her family's recipe using flour and butter. A formidable little Turkish crumble.

Preparation time: 30 minutes
Cooking time: 25 minutes
Resting time: overnight
For lots of friends – again
200 g (7 oz/scant 1 cup) caster (superfine) sugar
1 tablespoon lemon juice
200 g (7 oz) butter
200 g (7 oz/1⅓ cups) plain (all-purpose) flour
a good handful of crushed walnuts or whole pine nuts

First, make a syrup. Put the sugar and 125 ml (4 fl oz/½ cup) water in a small saucepan. Place the saucepan over low heat, and stir until the sugar has dissolved. Bring to the boil, still stirring, and skim off any white froth that forms on the surface. Add the lemon juice and continue to cook, stirring, for a further 3 minutes. Set aside to cool. Melt the butter in a saucepan over low heat. Add the flour, little by little, stirring until you have a roux and the taste of the flour has been cooked out (allow about 10 minutes). Add the nuts, continue stirring for 1 minute, then carefully add the syrup (watch out for spatter). Stir again, then cover and continue cooking over very low heat for 5 minutes. Spread and pat down the still-hot paste on a plate or in a small tin, and cut the helva into diamonds or small squares. Leave to chill in the refrigerator overnight. Serve cold, cut into small squares.

Note: This recipe is for a crunchy un helvası. For a softer version, turn off the heat after mixing the sugar into the mixture.

SEMOLINA HELVA
irmik helvası

A recipe that takes time (to cook the semolina on the heat) and attention (so you do not burn it!) and, in the end, a flavour with a hint of toasted grain and caramel.

Preparation time: 1 hour 10 minutes
Serves 6–8 friends
100 g (3½ oz) butter
200 g (7 oz/generous 1 cup) fine
or medium semolina
40 g (1½ oz/¼ cup) pine nuts
190 g (6¾ oz/scant 1 cup) caster
(superfine) sugar
400 ml (14 fl oz) milk
ground cinnamon for dusting

Melt the butter in a medium, heavy-based saucepan, add the semolina and pine nuts, and stir over very low heat for 45 minutes (yes, that long). The semolina will take on a caramel colour; make sure that it does not burn. Dissolve the sugar in the cold milk, and add to the semolina, still stirring. Once the first blisters appear on the surface, run a fork quickly through the semolina several times, to separate the grains – as if you wanted to stripe it – still over low heat. Remove from the heat (the semolina will be compact), divide the mixture between ramekins or small bowls, and wait for it to cool completely. Unmould and dust with cinnamon before serving.

RICE PUDDING
sütlaç

In Turkey, rice pudding is often quite runny. For a thicker or thinner consistency, vary the amount of cornflour added to the mixture.

Preparation time: 5 minutes
Cooking time: 40 minutes
Resting time: at least 4 hours
Serves 4
50 g (1¾ oz/¼ cup) short-grain rice
500 ml (17 fl oz/2 cups) milk
1 generous tablespoon cornflour (cornstarch)
65 g (2¼ oz/scant ⅓ cup) caster (superfine) sugar
ground cinnamon, to decorate

Cook the rice in a medium saucepan according to the packet instructions. Drain if needed. Heat the milk in a separate, clean medium saucepan, and add the rice when the first small bubbles appear in the milk. Stir for 5 minutes over medium heat, then add the cornflour, diluted in 1 tablespoon water to make a paste, and the sugar. Continue cooking, stirring constantly, for as long as it takes for the milk to thicken (about 15 minutes). Pour the rice pudding into a dish or several individual ramekins, and sprinkle with cinnamon. Once the rice pudding has cooled completely, chill in the refrigerator for at least 4 hours before serving.

DOUGHNUT BALLS
lokma

These sweet little puffs keep for a few days,
if stored in an airtight container.

Preparation time: 10 minutes
Resting time: at least 4 hours
Cooking time: 30 minutes
Serves 4
30 g (1 oz) potato starch
250 g (9 oz/1⅔ cups) strong flour
10 g (¼ oz) fresh yeast or scant 1 teaspoon dried
sunflower or other vegetable oil for deep-frying

SYRUP (ABOUT 300 ML/10½ FL OZ)
300 g (10½ oz/1⅓ cups) caster (superfine) sugar
1 tablespoon lemon juice

First, make the syrup. Put the sugar and 150 ml (5 fl oz) water in a small saucepan, and stir until the sugar has dissolved. Place the saucepan over medium heat. Bring the syrup mixture to the boil, still stirring, and skim off any white froth that forms on the surface. Add the lemon juice and continue to cook, stirring, for a further 3 minutes. Set aside to cool. To make the dough, blend the potato starch into 250 ml (9 fl oz/1 cup) water in a small bowl. Gradually mix the starchy water into the flour in a large bowl (making sure to avoid lumps). Blend the yeast into a little lukewarm water, and add it to the dough. Mix together. You should get a mixture like a thick crêpe batter (if it is too thick, add a little – a very little – hot water). Wrap the bowl in a damp tea towel (dish towel), and set aside in a warm place for at least 4 hours (the dough will rise). In a heavy-based saucepan, heat enough oil for deep-frying until it reaches 170°C (325°F), or a cube of bread dropped into the oil turns golden brown in 20 seconds (gently – definitely not too hot). Take some dough in your hand, gently squeeze your fist closed and, using a small spoon dipped in cold oil, remove the little 1 cm (½ inch) ball of dough that has squeezed up out of your fist and add it to the gently shimmering oil. Keep working like this, dropping several balls carefully into the oil until you have a batch; take care not to overcrowd the pan, so that the temperature of the oil remains even. Stir the balls in the oil for 1–2 minutes until they are golden brown all over. Remove carefully with a slotted spoon to a plate lined with paper towel, before dipping them in the syrup. Continue working in batches until all the dough has been used and all the doughnut balls are coated in the syrup.

PUMPKIN DESSERT

kabak tatlısı

Even better with a serving of kaymak (see page 216). Buffalo cream has the knack of mellowing the sweetness of fruit desserts. This dessert is traditionally eaten cold, but I am fond of it warm.

Preparation time: 5 minutes
Cooking time: 20 minutes
Serves 4
800 g (1 lb 12 oz) pumpkin (winter squash)
60 g (2¼ oz) butter
160 g (5¾ oz/¾ cup) caster (superfine) sugar
60 g (2¼ oz/½ cup) chopped walnuts

Peel the pumpkin, remove the seeds, and cut the flesh into slices about 3 cm (1¼ inches) thick. Melt the butter in a large frying pan over high heat, add the pumpkin and gently sauté for 1 minute. Pour over the sugar, reduce the heat slightly and cover the pan. Cook the pumpkin for 20 minutes, turning the slices halfway through. Allow to cool. Sprinkle with the walnuts just before serving.

BAKED QUINCE
ayva tatlısı

The quince is an odd fruit,
inedible raw but exceptionally
subtle and perfumed once
cooked. Depending on how
it is made, this dessert can
be almost like a quince jelly.
I prefer the version at the
Sakarya Tatlıcısı pâtisserie
at the Balık Pazarı (fish market)
in Beyoğlu, which is not as
sweet as some examples and
more balanced.

Preparation time: 10 minutes
Cooking time: 3 hours
Serves 4
2 quinces
**200 g (7 oz/scant 1 cup) caster
(superfine) sugar**
2 cloves (optional)

Peel the quinces and cut in half; remove
the core and keep the seeds. Place the
quince halves in a large saucepan, and
pour in enough water to reach the top
of the fruit. Add the sugar, quince seeds
and cloves (if using). Cook, covered,
over medium heat for 1 hour. Preheat
the oven to 120°C (235°F). After the
quinces have been cooking for an hour,
transfer them to a bain-marie (a dish set
inside another container filled with hot
water, so that it comes halfway up the
sides of the first dish). Bake in the oven
for 2 hours, topping up the hot water
in the bain-marie as needed. Remove
from the oven and allow to cool. Serve
cold, topped with kaymak (see note on
page 216) or crème fraîche.

SEMOLINA CAKE
irmik revani

The Middle Eastern version of a yoghurt cake, with
its traditional added twist of lemony flavour.

Preparation time: 10 minutes
Cooking time: 35 minutes
Serves 8
125 g (4½ oz) Turkish or Greek-style yoghurt
150 ml (5 fl oz) sunflower oil
2 eggs
50 g (1¾ oz/scant ¼ cup) caster (superfine) sugar
50 g (1¾ oz/⅓ cup) plain (all-purpose) flour
150 g (5½ oz/¾ cup) fine semolina
2 teaspoons baking powder
grated zest of 1 lemon

SYRUP (ABOUT 150 ML/5 FL OZ)
150 g (5½ oz/⅔ cup) caster (superfine) sugar
1 tablespoon lemon juice

First, make the syrup. Put the sugar and 100 ml (3½ fl oz) water in a small
saucepan, and stir until the sugar has dissolved. Place the saucepan over
medium heat. Bring the syrup mixture to the boil, still stirring, and skim
off any white froth that forms on the surface. Add the lemon juice and
continue to cook, stirring, for a further 3 minutes. Set aside. Preheat
the oven to 180°C (350°F). Using an electric mixer, mix together all the
cake ingredients. Pour the batter into a 25 cm (10 inch) round cake tin
or a 30 x 20 cm (12 x 8 inch) rectangular tin, and bake in the oven for
30 minutes until golden. When the cake comes out of the oven, pour
the cold syrup over the hot cake while still in the tin. Serve cold.

N⊕-BAKE CHOCOLATE CAKE
mozaik pasta

Chocolate may not be a traditional ingredient in Turkish desserts, but in Istanbul you often find this mosaik cake, made from chocolate and crushed biscuits and served with coffee. I came across it at the chef school restaurant in Kadir Has University, and I still remember it. Use very good, very fresh eggs, as they are not cooked in the recipe.

Preparation time: 10 minutes
Resting time: overnight
Serves 8
400 g (14 oz) Petit Beurre biscuits (cookies) or other plain sweet butter biscuits
2 eggs
2 generous tablespoons caster (superfine) sugar
3 tablespoons unsweetened cocoa powder
100 g (3½ oz/⅔ cup) chocolate chips (optional)
125 g (4½ oz) unsalted butter, melted and cooled
125 ml (4 fl oz/½ cup) milk

Break each of the biscuits into four pieces by hand. Set aside. Beat the eggs with the sugar, cocoa and chocolate chips (if using) in a large bowl. Add the melted butter and the milk, then gently fold in the biscuits, being careful not to crush them. Line the inside of a narrow loaf (bar) tin (about 27 x 9 x 7 cm/10¾ x 3½ x 2¾ inches) with a large piece of plastic wrap, carefully pour in the mixture and pack down well; cover with another layer of plastic wrap. Leave to chill in the refrigerator overnight – or even in the freezer for 2–3 hours before serving – so that the cake is quite firm.

CAN
City wanderer,
Tooistanbul

Franco-Turkish Can grew up dividing his time between Paris and Istanbul. After studying in the United States, he chose to settle in the City of Cities. Why? Because it is vast, attractive and endearing in its contrasts, and because its boundless dynamism makes room for things to happen. In 2013 he and his partner, Antoine, launched the blog, Tooistanbul – an insider's guide to the city. They organise culinary walking tours on both sides of the Bosphorus and their aim is to tell the story of their city as they live it and love it, using their tastebuds as their guide.

www.tooistanbul.com

SAHLEP

Sahlep arrives on Istanbul's menu with winter and is announced loudly by vendors all over the city: 'Sa-a-a-ahlep!' A hot, thick milk beverage flavoured with wild orchid powder, it is supposed to have fortifying and even aphrodisiac properties. It is difficult to track down outside of Turkey (for environmental reasons, as the exploitation of this wild plant has endangered the species to the point where it is now illegal to export it). You can, however, find ready-to-use sahlep mixes in Turkish or other Middle Eastern food shops and markets.

Preparation time: 2 minutes
Cooking time: 5 minutes
Makes 1 cup
1 teaspoon orchid powder
1 teaspoon cornflour (cornstarch)
250 ml (9 fl oz/1 cup) full-cream milk
granulated sugar, to taste
ground cinnamon

Blend the orchid powder and cornflour in a little of the milk. Pour the rest of the milk into a saucepan, add the flavoured milk and stir over low heat until the milk develops a creamy consistency. Pour the piping hot milk into a large cup, add sugar to taste and sprinkle with a little cinnamon.

LEM🍋NADE
limonata

A fresh lemonade on the shaded terrace of a chic café in Nişantaşi, after a long walk in the spring weather, and you will soon be off again on your tour of the local shops and markets. A good variation is to add a few mint leaves to the lemons for squeezing, or at the bottom of the lemonade glass, crushed using a pestle.

Preparation time: 10 minutes
Resting time: 1 hour
Makes 1.5 litres (52 fl oz/6 cups) lemonade
5 unwaxed lemons
200 g (7 oz/scant 1 cup) caster (superfine) sugar

Cut the unpeeled lemons into cubes, put in a medium–large bowl and cover them with the sugar. Leave to rest for at least 1 hour if possible, so that the lemons become impregnated with the sugar. Tip the contents of the bowl into a sieve set over a large bowl, then pour 1.5 litres (52 fl oz/6 cups) water in several lots over the fruit in the sieve, squeezing the lemon cubes with your hand to extract the juice. Once you have poured all the water through and the lemons are well squeezed out, set the lemonade aside in the refrigerator. Serve iced!

ISTANBUL, THE COCKTAIL

Istanbul *is* a cocktail: a fine mix of styles, the new and the old. **Müzedechanga**, a pioneering restaurant of the new Turkish cuisine, has created a rakı cocktail named after the city. It's best enjoyed on their terrace overlooking the Bosphorus. Thank you to Tarık Beyazıt for passing it on to me.

Preparation time: 5 minutes
Makes 1 glass
½ mandarin*, cut into 5 wedges
20 ml (1 fl oz) sugar syrup
40 ml (2 fl oz) vodka
20 ml (1 fl oz) rakı
20 ml (1 fl oz) lemon juice
crushed ice

Use a pestle to crush the pieces of mandarin with the sugar syrup in a cocktail shaker. Add the vodka, rakı, lemon juice and a big handful of crushed ice. Close the shaker, shake vigorously and serve in a pretty glass.

*At Müzedechanga, the mandarins used to come from Bodrum, a city in the southwest of Turkey, and have a very particular flavour and appearance (green outside, orange inside). It may be a little hard to justify going to Bodrum for a cocktail, so you can replace them with ordinary mandarins or bitter Seville oranges.

APPENDICES
INGREDIENTS AND RECIPE INDEX

PASTRIES AND CONDIMENTS

1: honey
2: yufka pastry
3: pomegranate molasses
4: sesame paste (tahini)
5: olive oil

6: Mild Turkish chilli paste (tatlı biber salçası)
7: grape molasses (pekmez)
8: angel hair pastry (kadayif)

GRAINS AND PULSES

1: chickpeas
2: fine semolina
3: haricot (navy) beans
4: split red lentils

5: rice
6: broad beans
7: burghul (bulgur)
8: black-eyed peas

FRESH HERBS

1: dill
2: mint
3: flat-leaf (Italian) parsley

DRIED HERBS AND SPICES

1: wild orchid powder (sahlep)
2: ground allspice
3: ground cinnamon
4: ground cumin
5: paprika
6: mastic gum (sakız)
7: pul biber (Aleppo pepper)

8: dried oregano
9: sumac
10: dried thyme
11: dried mint

TEA, COFFEE, RAKI

1: loose black tea
2: raki (an anise-flavoured liqueur)
3: Turkish coffee

DAIRY PRODUCTS

1: çeçil peynir (Turkish white cheese)
2 & 3: beyaz peynir (Turkish white cheese)
4: Turkish yoghurt

VEGETABLES

1: capsicum (pepper) and mild chillies
2: olives
3: samphire
4: vine leaves

5: purslane
6: fresh and dried chillies
7: eggplant (aubergine)

DRIED FRUIT, NUTS AND SEEDS

1: golden and black sesame seeds
2: whole and ground walnuts
3: dried apricots
4: whole and ground pistachio nut kernels

5: whole and ground almonds
6: pine nuts
7: dark and golden raisins

RECIPE INDEX

BREAKFAST

Simit and Turkish tea 12
Plain milk buns 14
Stuffed flatbread 16
Fried eggs and sucuk 18
Scrambled eggs with vegetables 20
Turkish coffee 22

THE TABLE OF THE MEYHANE

Pickles 30
Eggplant purée 32
Antakya spicy purée 34
'Spicy paste' 36
Chopped salad with walnuts 40
Yoghurt with cucumber 42
Parsley salad 44
Chickpea pockets 46
Didem's broad beans 48
Samphire salad with almonds 49
Garlic yoghurt 50
Eggplant with yoghurt 52
Cured bonito 54
Garlic and walnut purée 56
Broad bean purée 58
Purslane salad with yoghurt 60
Turkish tabouleh 62
Black-eyed pea salad 64
Agora squid with sauce 66
Mussel fritters 68
Fried anchovies 70
Marinated sea bass 72
Octopus salad 73
Sea bass stew 74
Mussel pilaki 76

SOUPS, MEATS AND RICE

Lentil soup 84
Chicken soup 86
Tripe soup 88
Tomato soup 90
Yoghurt soup 92
Meatballs 94
Steak tartare 95
'Lady's thighs' 96
Beef dumplings 98
Spicy mutton kebabs 100
Veal with tomato 102
Eggplant kebabs 103
Sautéed lamb with smoky eggplant 104
Lamb kebabs 108
Veal kebabs 110
Chicken wings 112
Sautéed lamb's liver 114
Lamb stew 116
Spinach with rice 118
Rice pilav and rice with vermicelli 120
Tomato pilav 122
Burghul pilav 124
Chicken pilav 126
Sea bass pilav 128

AT HOME

Zucchini fritters 136
Artichoke hearts in olive oil 138
Burghul balls 140
Sautéed eggplant and capsicum 142
Fried vegetable salad 144
Lentil balls 146
Aicha's salad 148
Haricot beans and lamb in
a tomato sauce 150
Haricot bean salad 152
Black-eyed peas with tomato 154
Braised celery 156
Braised zucchini 158
Leeks in olive oil 160
Vine leaves 162

Flat bean salad 166
Börek 168
Little börek from Delicatessen 170
Stuffed vegetables 174
Eggplants with meat 176

STREET FOOD

Islak burger 186
Turkish pizza 190
Pide 192
Fish sandwich 196
Stuffed potatoes 198
Tripe sandwich 199
Stuffed mussels 200
Wrap 202
Yoghurt 204
Ayran 204

TURKISH DELIGHTS

Baklava 214
Cheese pastry 216
Pistachio kadayif 218
Vanilla milk pudding 220
Crème brûlée 222
Choux fritters in syrup 224
Shortbreads 226
Savoury sesame biscuits 228
Mastic Turkish delight 234
Almond helva 238
Flour helva 240
Semolina helva 241
Rice pudding 242
Doughnut balls 244
Pumpkin dessert 246
Baked quince 247
Semolina cake 248
No-bake chocolate cake 250
Sahlep 254
Lemonade 256
Istanbul, the cocktail 257

INDEX

ALMOND
almond helva 238
samphire salad with almonds 49
sea bass pilav 128
shortbreads 226

BEEF
beef dumplings 98
eggplant kebabs 103
eggplant with meat 176
islak burger 186
'lady's thighs' 96
lahmaçun 190
meatballs 94
meat sarma 162
minced meats wrap 202
spicy mutton kebabs 100
spinach with rice 118
steak tartare 95
stuffed vegetables 174

BEETROOT
pickles 30
Turkish tabouleh 62

BROAD BEANS
broad bean purée 58
Didem's broad beans 48

BURGHUL
burghul balls 140
burghul pilav 124
steak tartare 95
Turkish tabouleh 62
veal kebabs 110

CAPSICUM
chopped salad with walnuts 40
fried vegetable salad 144
octopus salad 73
pickles 30
sautéed eggplant and capsicum .. 142
scrambled eggs with vegetables ... 20
'spicy paste' 36
stuffed vegetables 174

CARROT
Aicha's salad 148

CHEESE
cheese börek 168
cheese filling 16
cheese pastry 216
cheese pide 192
milk buns with cheese 14
sautéed lamb with
smoky eggplant 104
stuffed potatoes 198

CHICKEN
chicken pide 192
chicken pilav 126
chicken soup 86
chicken wings 112
chicken wrap 202

CHICKPEAS
chickpea pockets 46
pickles 30

CHOCOLATE
no-bake chocolate cake 250

CINNAMON
baklava 214
chicken pilav 126
chickpea pockets 46
eggplant with meat 176
'Lady's thighs' 96
leeks in olive oil 160
rice pudding 242

sahlep 254
semolina helva 241
stuffed mussels 200

CUCUMBER
chopped salad with walnuts 40
pickles 30
yoghurt with cucumber 42

CUMIN
chicken wrap 202
lentil balls 146
meatballs 94
veal kebabs 110

CURRANTS
chicken pilav 126
chickpea pockets 46
simple sarma 162

DRIED PULSES
black-eyed pea salad 64
black-eyed peas with tomato 154
haricot bean salad 152
haricot beans and lamb 150
lentil balls 146
lentil soup 84

EGG
fried eggs and sucuk 18
scrambled eggs with vegetables ... 20

EGGPLANT
eggplant kebabs 103
eggplant purée 32
eggplant with meat 176
eggplant with yoghurt 52
fried vegetable salad 144
sautéed eggplant and capsicum . 142
sautéed lamb with
smoky eggplant 104
stuffed vegetables 174

FISH AND SEAFOOD
agora squid with sauce 66
cured bonito 54
fish sandwich 196
fried anchovies 70
marinated sea bass 72
mussel fritters 68
mussel pilaki 76
octopus salad 73
sea bass pilav 128
sea bass stew 74
stuffed mussels 200

FLAT BEANS
flat bean salad 166

FRUIT
baked quince 247
lemonade 256

GARLIC
garlic and walnut purée 56
garlic yoghurt 50
pickles 30

HERBS
milk buns with herbs 14
parsley salad 44

KADAYIF
cheese pastry 216
pistachio kadayif 218

LAMB
flat bean salad (winter) 166
haricot beans and lamb 150
lahmaçun 190
lamb kebabs 108
lamb stew 116

sautéed lamb with
smoky eggplant 104
wrap 202

MASTIC
crème brûlée 222
mastic Turkish delight 234

MILK
crème brûlée 222
milk buns with cheese 14
milk buns with herbs 14
plain milk buns 14
rice pudding 242
sahlep 254
vanilla milk pudding 220

MOLASSES
Antaya spicy purée 34
fish sandwich 196
parsley salad 44
sautéed lamb's liver 114
simit 12
'spicy paste' 36
Turkish tabouleh 62

MUTTON
eggplant kebabs 103
meat sarma 162
spicy mutton kebabs 100
stuffed vegetables 174

OFFAL
sautéed lamb's liver 114
tripe sandwich 199
tripe soup 88

PAPRIKA
pickles 30
sautéed lamb's liver 114
sautéed lamb with
smoky eggplant 104
veal with tomato 102

PINE NUTS
chicken pilav 126
chickpea pockets 46
flour helva 240
mussel fritters 68
sea bass pilav 128
simple sarma 162
stuffed mussels 200

PISTACHIOS
baklava 214
pistachio kadayif 218
sea bass pilav 128
vanilla milk pudding 220
veal kebabs 110

POTATO
chickpea pockets 46
mussel pilaki 76
potato filling 16
stuffed potatoes 198

RICE
chicken pilav 126
rice pudding 242
rice with vermicelli 120
sea bass pilav 128
spinach with rice 118
stuffed mussels 200
stuffed vegetables 174
tomato pilav 122
yoghurt soup 92

SAMPHIRE
samphire salad with almonds 49

SEMOLINA
almond helva 238
semolina cake 248
semolina helva 241

SESAME SEEDS
milk buns with cheese 14
milk buns with herbs 14
plain milk buns 14
savoury sesame biscuits 228
simit 12

SPINACH
börek with spinach 168
Little börek from Delicatessen 170
pide with spinach 192
spinach filling 16
spinach with rice 118

SUMAC
parsley salad 44
'spicy paste' 36

TAHINI
almond helva 238
chickpea pockets 46

TOMATO
Antaya spicy purée 34
chopped salad with walnuts 40
mussel pilaki 76
scrambled eggs with vegetables ... 20
'spicy paste' 36
stuffed vegetables 174
tomato pilav 122
tomato soup 90
veal with tomato 102

VINE LEAVES
sarma 162

VEAL
veal kebabs 110
veal with tomato 102

VERMICELLI
chicken soup 86
rice with vermicelli 120

WALNUTS
Antaya spicy purée 34
baklava 214
chopped salad with walnuts 40
Didem's broad beans 48
flour helva 240
garlic and walnut purée 56
mussel fritters 68
parsley salad 44
pumpkin dessert 246
shortbreads 226
'spicy paste' 36

YOGHURT
ayran 204
eggplant with yoghurt 52
garlic yoghurt 50
purslane salad with yoghurt 60
yoghurt soup 92
yoghurt with cucumber 42

YUFKA
baklava 214
börek 168
Little börek from Delicatessen 170

ZUCCHINI
Aicha's salad 148
braised zucchini 158
fried vegetable salad 144
stuffed vegetables 174
zucchini fritters 136

ADDRESS BOOK

Walk around Taksim (and further north)

Taksim Square, islak burger, döner kebab, fresh juice: right at the top of the two avenues going up the hill from Pera that open onto the square (Istiklâl and Sıraselviler Caddesi).

Hala, mantı restaurant: Büyük Parmakkapı Çukurluçeşme Sokak No: 14/A, Beyoğlu.

Zübeyir Ocakbaşı, grill restaurant: Şehit Muhtar Mahallesi, Bekar Sokak No: 28.

In the Şişli neighbourhood:

Hünkar, lokanta: Mim Kemal Öke Caddesi No: 21.

Kantin, restaurant and delicatessen: Akkavak Sokak No: 30.

Kürşat Ayvalık Zeytinyaği, olive oils: Şakayık Sokaka No: 75/B.

Damla Doudurma Boza, artisanal ice creams: Kurtuluş Caddesi No: 110/A.

In the Beşiktaş neighbourhood:

Kafadaroğlu, baklava, börek: Ortabahçe Caddesi No: 21/G.

7/8 Hasanpaşa Fırını, bakery: Sinanpaşa Mh., Şehit Asım Caddesi No: 12.

Abusta 33 Mersin Tantuni, lahmaçun, tantuni: Sinanpaşa Mahallesi Kazan Sokak No: 7/B.

Karadeniz Döner, döner kebab: Sinanpaşa Mahallesi, Mumcu Bakkal Sokak No: 6.

Beşiktaş covered market, Saturdays: Nüzhetiye Caddesi.

Neighbouring quarter of Ortaköy: for its famous kumpir, in a neighbourhood devoted to it, behind the very beautiful Ortaköy Mosque.

Further north, in the Emirgan neighbourhood, **Müzedechanga**, restaurant, bar, terrace (unique), museum (Sakıp Sabancı Müzesi, next door): Emirgan Mahallesi, Sakıp Sabancı Caddesi No: 42.

Walk in Pera
(Karaköy, Pera, Çukurcuma, Cihangir)

In the Karaköy neighbourhood:

Namli, restaurant, breakfast: Rıhtim Caddesi No: 1/1.

Lokanta Maya, restaurant: Kemankeş Caddesi No: 35/A. Just next door (No: 37/A), **Karaköy Lokantası**, restaurant.

Galata Simitçisi, bakery: Mumhane Caddesi No: 47/A.

In the Pera neighbourhood:

Pera Palas, palace, tea salon (and mastic macarons): Meşrutiyet Caddesi No: 52, Tepebaşı.

Yakup, meyhane: Asmalı Mescit Caddesi No: 21/B. Just opposite (No: 16), another very famous meyhane: **Asmalı Cavit**.

Sakarya Tatlıcısı, artisanal pâtisserie: Dudu Odaları Sokak No: 3, Balık Pazarı.

Saray, pâtisserie: Istiklâl Caddesi No: 105, or, a little further along the pedestrian thoroughfare, **Hacı Bekir**, Turkish delight (No: 83/A).

In the Cihangir neighbourhood:

Balya Organik, restaurant and organic grocer: Defterdar Yokuşu, Batarya Sokak No: 16.

Van Kahvaltı Evi, breakfast: Defterdar Yokuşu No: 52/A.

Asri Turşucu, pickles: Ağahamam Sokak No: 9/A.

Kücük Kurabiye Dükkani, home-made cakes: Oba Sokak.

Walk on the Asian side

Bingöl Bal Pazarı, honeys: Selmanağa çeşme Sokak No: 1, Üsküdar.

Kanaat Lokantası, lokanta: Selmanipak Caddesi No: 9, Üsküdar.

Aytekin Erol, Turkish delight, helva and little sweets (candies): Atlas Sokak No: 21, Balıkçılar Çarşısı, Üsküdar.

Kadıköy Market (Tarihi Salı Pazarı), Tuesdays and Thursdays: Hasanpaşa Mahallesi, Mandıra Caddesi No: 1.

Walk in old Istanbul (Fatih)

Agora Meyhanesi 1890, meyhane: Mürselpaşa Caddesi No: 185, Ayvansaray.

Asitane, restaurant: Kariye Camii Sokak No: 6, Edirnekapı.

Chef School apprentice restaurant, restaurant and school: Kadir Has Caddesi Cibali.

Ucuzcular, spices (Egyptian Bazaar): Mısır Çarşısı İçi No: 51.

Kurukahveci Mehmet Efendi, coffee roaster: Tahmis Sokak No: 66, Eminönü.

Café Ethem Tezçakar, café (Grand Bazaar): Hacıcılar Caddesi No: 61/63.

Abdulla, bath products, soaps (Grand Bazaar): Hacıcılar Caddesi No: 58/60

Sultanahmet köftecisi, cafeteria (köfte): Divanyolu Caddesi No: 12/A, Sultanahmet.

The market gardens of Yedikule: in the southwest of Fatih, at the foot of the old fortress walls, from the Yedikulekapı to Topkapı.

The neighbourhood of Samatya (for its little grilled fish restaurants): beside the Sea of Marmara, in the city's south.

ABOUT THE AUTHOR

Author Pomme Larmoyer is a food writer, editor and traveller. She believes you can learn everything you need to know about a country from its kitchens and enjoys talking with other people from other cultures about their style of food.

THANK YOU

The best of Istanbul is in the people of Istanbul. Thanks to those who wrote this book.

Thanks to Rosemarie and Marabout for their trust.

Thanks to Akiko, Sabrina and Pierre for their sharp eyes, curiosity and enthusiasm when faced with a plate of kaymak, among other things. Thanks to Audrey. Thanks to Zeina, and long may the drawing live on.

Thanks to Ayşe for being my Turkish cooking teacher with such rare energy, willingness, clarity and kindness.

Thanks to Annie for opening her Armenian recipe notebooks for me and answering my questions with incredible patience and generosity.

Thanks to Hande Bozdoğan for her unhesitating welcome, her advice, encouragement and goodwill. Thanks to Ezel Akay (**Agora Meyhanesi**), Didem Şenol (**Lokanta Maya**), Elif Yalın (**Delicatessen**), Tarık Beyazıt (**Changa**) and their teams, whom received us like royalty; it is very good to be your guests.

Thanks to Antoine, Can and Tooistanbul for lending us the keys to their city, for their lively, personal walking itineraries and their precious help.

Thanks to everyone who threw open the doors of their shops, back rooms, workshops, kitchens, restaurants and schools for us. A thousand thanks: to the whole team at **Van Kahvaltı Evi**, to the Asri Turşucu brothers (the pickles!) and the **Kafadaroğlu** ones (baklava), to the friends from **Abusta 33 Mersin Tantuni** (the lahmaçun), to **Aytekin Erol** and his accomplice **Kemal Çamlıca** (ah, the lokum!), to chef Bugra and the whole team at the **chef school apprentice restaurant** at Kadir Has University, and to the team at **Zübeyir Ocakbaşı**.

In Paris, Rue du Faubourg-Saint-Denis, thanks to the team at **Urfa Dürüm** for their lesson in street food. Thanks as well to Samuel Yafamis and the team at **Istanbul Pizza Grill**.

Thanks to Emel, Nurdane and Ana for taking the time to share their family recipes and stories.

Thanks to Nihal and Aylin for initiating me into their immense culinary culture – thanks also for allowing me to discover mastic macarons.

Thanks to Sophie Malié and Sophie my sister, who helped me to encounter, discover, move forwards. Thanks to Oruç, Senay and Guillaume Perrier.

Thanks to Cyril for tasting everything as planned and for holding my hand in the plane and in the Istanbul we both love.

For everything, *teşekkür* Istanbul.

Published in 2023 by Murdoch Books, an imprint of Allen & Unwin
First published by Marabout in 2015

Murdoch Books Australia
Cammeraygal Country
83 Alexander Street
Crows Nest NSW 2065
Phone: +61 (0)2 8425 0100
murdochbooks.com.au
info@murdochbooks.com.au

Murdoch Books UK
Ormond House
26–27 Boswell Street
London WC1N 3JZ
Phone: +44 (0) 20 8785 5995
murdochbooks.co.uk
info@murdochbooks.co.uk

For corporate orders and custom publishing, contact our business development
team at salesenquiries@murdochbooks.com.au

Publisher: Corinne Roberts, Jane Morrow
Designer: Chimène Denneulin
Editor: Siobhan O'Connor
Photographers: Akiko Ida, Pierre Javelle
Illustrator: Zeina Abirached
Stylist: Sabrina Fauda-Rôle
Translator: Melissa McMahon
Production director: Lou Playfair

Text and design © Hachette Livre (Marabout) 2015
The moral right of the author has been asserted.

Murdoch Books acknowledges the Traditional Owners of the Country on which we live and work.
We pay our respects to all Aboriginal and Torres Strait Islander Elders, past and present.

ISBN 978 1 92261 699 9

A catalogue record for this
book is available from the
NATIONAL LIBRARY OF AUSTRALIA
National Library of Australia

A catalogue record for this book is available from the British Library.

Colour reproduction by Splitting Image Colour Studio Pty Ltd, Wantirna, Victoria
Printed by 1010 Printing International Limited, China

OVEN GUIDE: You may find cooking times vary depending on the oven you are using. For fan-forced
ovens, as a general rule, set the oven temperature to 20°C (35°F) lower than indicated in the recipe.

IMPORTANT: Those who might be at risk from the effects of salmonella poisoning (the elderly, pregnant
women, young children and those suffering from immune deficiency diseases) should consult their doctor
with any concerns about eating raw eggs.

10 9 8 7 6 5 4 3 2 1